SPANISH GRAMMAR REVISION

Punto por Punto

NEIL CREIGHTON

Nelson

Thomas Nelson and Sons Ltd
Nelson House Mayfield Road
Walton-on-Thames Surrey
KT12 5PL UK

Nelson Blackie
Wester Cleddens Road
Bishopbriggs
Glasgow G64 2NZ UK

Thomas Nelson (Hong Kong) Ltd
Toppan Building 10/F
22a Westlands Road
Quarry Bay Hong Kong

Thomas Nelson Australia
102 Dodds Street
South Melbourne
Victoria 3205 Australia

Nelson Canada
1120 Birchmount Road
Scarborough Ontario
M1K 5G4 Canada

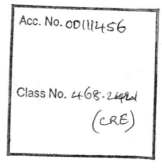
First published by Thomas Nelson and Sons Ltd 1986

I(T)P Thomas Nelson is an International
       Thomson Publishing Company.
I(T)P is used under licence.

ISBN 0-17-445088-5
NPN 10

Printed in Singapore

Foreword

Punto por Punto combines simplicity with comprehensiveness in the following ways:

- From the basics to the more advanced aspects of the Spanish language, each grammatical point is clearly explained in the following sections: The Ten Tenses; Pronouns and Adjectives; Points Alphabetically

- Examples from everyday Spanish illustrate each grammatical point

- Easy-to-read tables highlight the patterns in language and are a useful visual memory aid

- A comprehensive Table of Contents, numerous cross-references and a full index ensure ease of reference

The author has many years' experience of teaching secondary pupils and is currently Head of Modern Languages in a comprehensive school. He is the author of the successful *Mille et un Points*, Harrap's French Grammar Revision.

Contents

Introduction: Summary of Grammatical Terms; Abbreviations 1

PART THREE — POINTS ALPHABETICALLY

INDEX   The references are to page numbers

Summary of Grammatical Terms

1. Basic components of a sentence

Verbs: denote an action: hits, gives; or a state: is, seems.

Nouns:	things	abstractions	persons	places
e.g.	book	hour, idea	boy, Mary	coast, Madrid

Pronouns: sum up and replace a noun, e.g. it, them, he, her.

2. Constructing a sentence

	Subject	**VERB**	**Direct Object**	**Indirect Object**
Noun form	The man	**SOLD**	a radio	*to*★ the lady
Pronoun form	He	**SOLD**	it	*to*★ her

— **Subject:** performs the action: The **MAN** sold...
— **Direct Object:** answers the question *"What did he sell?"*...
  ...sold a **RADIO**.
— **Indirect Object:** the direction, destination of the object, usually introduced by *to* (and sometimes *for*, §12):
  ... a radio **TO THE LADY**.

★Note: In English, the *to* is often omitted, and the word order changed: The man sold [*to*] the lady a radio.
He sold it [*to*] her.

3. Other components

Adjectives: describe nouns: a **GOOD** book   the **SMALL** boy
Articles: indefinite article ──➚   definite article ──────➚
Adverbs: qualify ⎰ *verbs*   : I read **SLOWLY**
⎱ *adjectives*   : He is **VERY** lucky
other adverbs : He walks **EXTREMELY FAST**.

Conjunctions: (a) join words, e.g. **and, or, but** (§28)
(b) introduce clauses, e.g. **until** he comes (§62)

Prepositions: (a) precede nouns and pronouns and define position, direction, time, e.g. **under** the tree; **to** Madrid; **before** 2 o'clock (§50)
(b) link verbs to nouns and pronouns: *Resistió A la tentación* (§51);
and to infinitives: *Dejé DE preocuparme* (§40).

4. What is a clause? ...a sentence?

A clause is a group of words containing a *subject* and **verb**. If the clause makes complete sense it is a **SENTENCE**, or the **MAIN CLAUSE** among subordinate clauses in a longer sentence.

Main Clause	Subordinate Clauses	
I **finished** it	before *he* **came**	because *I* was **afraid**

5. More about the Verb

Tenses: refer to a point in time: **Past** ← **Present** → **Future** (§1 – 10)
Forms of the verb —
Affirmative: a positive statement   : You read it.
Negative: introduces not, etc. (§42) : You do **NOT** read it.
Interrogative: question form (§66)   : **Do you** read it?
Moods —
Indicative: The most usual pattern of the Ten Tenses (§1 – 10).
Subjunctive: Special tense patterns under certain conditions (§62).
Imperative: Commands, orders (§38)
Infinitive: English: TO speak, etc. Spanish: hablAR, vendER, vivIR.
Passive: The subject *suffers* (i.e. does not perform) an action:
The ring (subject) was examined by the jeweller (agent). (§46)
Reflexive: *"self"* implied: I got [myself] up. (§56)
Participles: *Past:*   e.g. workED: I have workED. (§6 and 47)
                   Present: e.g. workING: I am workING. (§52)

6. Agreement

(a) Adjectives, nouns and pronouns can vary in:
    gender: masculine/feminine; **number:** singular/plural (§22; 43)
(b) Subject-Verb agreement, e.g. I eat, he eatS. (§61)

ABBREVIATIONS

m. or **masc.**	= *masculine*	**fam.**	= *familiar*
f. or **fem.**	= *feminine*	**pol.**	= *polite*
s. or **sing.**	= *singular*	**R.C.V.**	= *radical changing verb*
pl. or **plur.**	= *plural*	**S.C.V.**	= *spelling change verb*
inv.	= *invariable* (i.e. no agreement)		

OTHER INDICATIONS

— **indicates** *an omission* in one language, but not necessarily in
   the other:
   El chico y la chica = The boy and __ girl.

[ ] **indicate:** (a) *literal meanings*, e.g. I get [myself] up. (§56)
                   (b) *an alternative rendering*, e.g.
                   Mis manos son más grandes que [las suyas] las de él. (§17)

Part One – The Ten Tenses

§1 THE PRESENT TENSE

A. MEANING

(yo) *hablo* may be translated into English as follows:
1. **I speak**
2. **I am speaking** — this "immediate" present may also be translated by *estar* + *present participle* (See §52)
3. **I do speak** — *do/does* is used in English in interrogative and negative forms, and for emphasis. The auxiliary *do/does* is never translated into Spanish.

B. FORMATION

1. **Regular verbs** — three conjugations, -ar, -er, -ir.

   (a) -ar type, hablar = *to speak*
   Remove **-ar,** *add the endings*

stem	endings	Corresponding subject pronouns
habl	**o**	yo
habl	**as**	tú
habl	**a**	él, ella, usted (Vd.)
habl	**amos**	nosotros, -as
habl	**áis**	vosotros, -as
habl	**an**	ellos, ellas, ustedes (Vds.)
stem	endings	See §11 for usage

   (b) -er type, vender = *to sell*
   Remove **-er,** *add the endings*
   vend **o**
   vend **es**
   vend **e**
   vend **emos**
   vend **éis**
   vend **en**

   (c) -ir type, vivir = *to live*
   Remove **-ir,** *add the endings*
   viv **o**
   viv **es**
   viv **e**
   viv **imos**
   viv **ís**
   viv **en**

2. **Radical changing verbs in the present tense**

-ar, -er, -ir	other -ir; -eír, -eñir	special cases	
e → ie	e → i	u → ue	i → ye
o → ue		i → ie	o → hue

(a) -ar, -er, -ir verbs

When the stress falls on the stem vowel **e** or **o**, radical (stem) changes take place as shown below.

Nosotros and *vosotros* stems remain unchanged.

e → ie				o → ue		
pensar	**perder**	**sentir**		**contar**	**volver**	**dormir**
to think	*to lose*	*to feel*		*to count*	*to return*	*to sleep*
piens o	pierd o	sient o		cuent o	vuelv o	duerm o
piens as	pierd es	sient es		cuent as	vuelv es	duerm es
piens a	pierd e	sient e		cuent a	vuelv e	duerm e
pens amos	perd emos	sent imos		cont amos	volv emos	dorm imos
pens áis	perd éis	sent ís		cont áis	volv éis	dorm ís
piens an	pierd en	sient en		cuent an	vuelv en	duerm en

Common examples

e ⟶ ie		o ⟶ ue	
-ar acertar	= to hit upon	**-ar** acordarse	= to remember
atravesar	= to cross	acostarse	= to go to bed
calentar	= to heat	almorzar	= to lunch
cerrar	= to close	aprobar	= to approve
comenzar	= to begin	consolar	= to console
confesar	= to confess	costar	= to cost
despertar(se)	= to wake (awaken)	encontrar	= to find
		forzar	= to force
empezar	= to begin	mostrar	= to show
enterrar	= to bury	probar	= to try, prove
manifestar	= to reveal	recordar	= to remind
merendar	= to have a snack	renovar	= to renew
negar	= to deny	sonar	= to sound
recomendar	= to recommend	soñar	= to dream
sentarse	= to sit down	volar	= to fly
temblar	= to tremble		
tentar	= to tempt		

e ⟶ ie		o ⟶ ue	
-er atender	= to attend to	**-er** doler	= to ache
defender	= to defend	morder	= to bite
encender	= to light	mover	= to move
tender	= to stretch	resolver	= to solve
verter	= to pour out	soler	= to be used to

e ⟶ ie	

-ir advertir = to warn
consentir = to consent
divertir(se) = to amuse(enjoy)
herir = to wound
hervir = to boil
mentir = to lie
preferir = to prefer
sugerir = to suggest
transferir = to transfer

o ⟶ ue	

-ir morir = to die

Radical changing weather verbs	
llover → **llue**ve	*It rains*
tronar → **true**na	*It thunders*
helar → **hie**la	*It freezes*
nevar → **nie**va	*It snows*
See §65, **Weather**	

Note: discernir (*to discern*) and **concernir** (*to concern*) also have the radical change **e → ie**, but only in the present tense. Concernir is a defective verb — it exists only in some third person singular forms.

(b) Other -ir; -eír, -eñir
The stressed stem vowel **e → i**.
Nosotros and *vosotros* stems remain unchanged.

-ir	-(g)ir and -(gu)ir:*see spelling changes below*		-eír	-eñir
pedir *to ask*	**corregir** *to correct*	**seguir** *to follow*	**reír** *to laugh*	**reñir** *to scold*
pid o	corri**J** o	si**G** o	rí o	riñ o
pid es	corrig es	sigu es	rí es	riñ es
pid e	corrig e	sigu e	rí e	riñ e
ped imos	correg imos	segu imos	re ímos	reñ imos
ped ís	correg ís	segu ís	re ís	reñ ís
pid en	corrig en	sigu en	rí en	riñ en

Common examples
-ir competir = to compete
despedir = to say good-bye
elegir(J) = to choose
impedir = to prevent
repetir = to repeat

-ir servir = to serve
vestir = to clothe
-eír freír = to fry
sonreír = to smile
-eñir teñir = to dye

(c) Special cases
Nosotros and *vosotros* stems remain unchanged.

u → ue	i → ie	i → ye	o → hue
jugar	**inquirir**	**errar**	**oler**
to play	*to inquire*	*to wander*	*to smell*
jueg o	inquier o	yerr o	huel o
jueg as	inquier es	yerr as	huel es
jueg a	inquier e	yerr a	huel e
jug amos	inquir imos	err amos	ol emos
jug áis	inquir ís	err áis	ol éis
jueg an	inquier en	yerr an	huel en

Like inquirir: adquirir = to acquire

(d) Some nouns and adjectives share these stem changes
nevar   = to snow .... la nieve   = snow
almorzar = to lunch .... el almuerzo = lunch
forzar   = to force .... la fuerza   = force
renovar = to renew .... el renuevo = renewal

3. Spelling changing verbs in the present tense.

(Also known as orthographic changing verbs)

(a) -er and -ir verbs
A consonant change occurs to preserve the same stem sound before the **o** of the **yo** form (and before **a** in the present subjunctive).

(i) -ger and -gir: G → J	
coger	**dirigir**
to seize	*to direct*
co**J** o	diri**J** o
cog es	dirig es
cog e	dirig e
cog emos	dirig imos
cog éis	dirig ís
cog en	dirig en

(ii) -guir: GU → G
distinguir
to distinguish
distin**G** o
distingu es
distingu e
distingu imos
distingu ís
distingu en

Note: some **-gir** and **-guir** verbs also undergo a radical change:
seguir → s**I**go *corregir* → corr**I**jo (See 2(b) above).

(iii) -quir: QU → C

delinquir
to transgress

delin**C**	o
delinqu	es
delinqu	e
delinqu	imos
delinqu	ís
delinqu	en

(iv) consonant + -cer and -cir: C → Z

ve**N**cer *to conquer*		espa**R**cir *to scatter*	
venZ	o	esparZ	o
venc	es	esparc	es
venc	e	esparc	e
venc	emos	esparc	imos
venc	éis	esparc	ís
venc	en	esparc	en

But: *vowel* + **-cer** and **-cir**: add **Z** before the **C** in the *yo* form which in fact changes the sound, unlike (iv) above when **Z** replaces the **C** to retain the same sound before the **o**.

Examples:
n**A**cer, *to be born*: na**Z**Co, naces, nace, etc.
obed**E**cer, *to obey*: obede**Z**Co, obedeces, obedece, etc.
con**O**cer, *to know*: cono**Z**Co, conoces, conoce, etc.
cond**U**cir, *to drive*: condu**Z**Co, conduces, conduce, etc.

Common verbs

aparecer	= to appear	introducir	= introduce
compadecer	= to pity	producir	= to produce
crecer	= to grow	reproducir	= to reproduce
merecer	= to deserve	traducir	= to translate
pertenecer	= to belong	lucir	= to shine

Note: c**O**cer, to boil (unlike *con**O**cer*) changes C → Z.
It is also radical changing:
cuezo, **cue**ces, **cue**ce, cocemos, cocéis, **cue**cen

(b) -uir verbs (not **-guir** verbs: see 3(a) above)
y is placed before any ending that does not begin with **i**.
Thus the *nosotros* and *vosotros* forms remain unchanged.

huir *to flee*		**argüir*** *to argue*	
hu**Y**	o	argu**Y**	o
hu**Y**	es	argu**Y**	es
hu**Y**	e	argu**Y**	e
hu	imos	argü*	imos
hu	ís	argü*	ís
hu**Y**	en	argu**Y**	en

Common examples

concluir	= to conclude
construir	= to build
contribuir	= to contribute
distribuir	= to distribute
excluir	= to exclude
incluir	= to include
substituir	= to substitute

*Diaeresis (¨) on the *infinitive* and *nosotros* and *vosotros* forms.

(c) -iar and -uar verbs

An **accent** is added to the **i** or **u**, except in the *nosotros* and *vosotros* forms

variar		**continuar**	
to vary		*to continue*	
varí	o	continú	o
varí	as	continú	as
varí	a	continú	a
vari	amos	continu	amos
vari	áis	continu	áis
varí	an	continú	an

Common examples

enviar	= to send
fiar	= to entrust
liar	= to bind
actuar	= to actuate
habituar	= to accustom
situar	=to situate
valuar	= to appraise

Note: The following verbs do *not* take an accent on the **i** or **u**:

acariciar	= to stroke	apaciguar	= to pacify
anunciar	= to announce	averiguar	= to ascertain
cambiar	= to change	evacuar	= to evacuate
envidiar	= to envy		
estudiar	= to study		
diferenciar	= to differentiate		
limpiar	= to clean		

(d) reunir, *to reunite*: accent added (except *nosotros/vosotros* forms)
reúno, reúnes, reúne, reunimos, reunís, reúnen.

4. Twenty verbs IRREGULAR in the Present Tense:

1. CABER *to fit in*	2. CAER *to fall*	3. DAR *to give*	4. DECIR *to say/tell*	5. ESTAR *to be*
quepo	caigo	doy	digo	estoy
cabes	caes	das	dices	estás
cabe	cae	da	dice	está
cabemos	caemos	damos	decimos	estamos
cabéis	caéis	dais	decís	estáis
caben	caen	dan	dicen	están
6. HABER★ *to have*	**7. HACER** *to do/make*	**8. IR** *to go*	**9. OÍR** *to hear*	**10. PODER** *to be able*
he	hago	voy	oigo	puedo
has	haces	vas	oyes	puedes
ha	hace	va	oye	puede
hemos	hacemos	vamos	oímos	podemos
habéis	hacéis	vais	oís	podéis
han	hacen	van	oyen	pueden
11. PONER *to put*	**12. QUERER** *to want/like*	**13. SABER** *to know*	**14. SALIR** *to go out*	**15. SER** *to be*
pongo	quiero	sé	salgo	soy
pones	quieres	sabes	sales	eres
pone	quiere	sabe	sale	es
ponemos	queremos	sabemos	salimos	somos
ponéis	queréis	sabéis	salís	sois
ponen	quieren	saben	salen	son
16. TENER *to have*	**17. TRAER** *to bring*	**18. VALER** *to be worth*	**19. VENIR** *to come*	**20. VER** *to see*
tengo	traigo	valgo	vengo	veo
tienes	traes	vales	vienes	ves
tiene	trae	vale	viene	ve
tenemos	traemos	valemos	venimos	vemos
tenéis	traéis	valéis	venís	veis
tienen	traen	valen	vienen	ven

★Haber, *to have*, is used to form the Compound Tenses, §6–10.
Also compounds, e.g.

decir :	*predecir*	= to predict	**tener** :	*retener*	= to keep
hacer :	*satisfacer*	= to satisfy	**traer** :	*distraer*	= to distract
poner :	*suponer*	= to suppose	**venir** :	*convenir*	= to agree, suit
salir :	*sobresalir*	= to excel			

§2 THE FUTURE TENSE

A. THE TRUE FUTURE

1. **Meaning:** I *shall/will* speak

2. **Formation: Stem + endings** (derived from the present tense of *haber*)

(a) REGULAR VERBS: -ar, -er, -ir
The **INFINITIVE** is used as **the STEM**

-AR	ENDINGS		AUXIL. VERB	
hablar	é	I	shall	speak
hablar	ás	You	will	speak
hablar	á	{He, she, You (pol.)	will	speak
hablar	emos	We	shall	speak
hablar	éis	You	will	speak
hablar	án	They, you (pol.)	will	speak
-ER				
vender	é	I	shall	sell
vender	ás	You	will	sell
vender	á	{He, she, You (pol.)	will	sell
vender	emos	We	shall	sell
vender	éis	You	will	sell
vender	án	They, you (pol.)	will	sell
-IR				
vivir	é	I	shall	live
vivir	ás	You	will	live
vivir	á	{He, she, You (pol.)	will	live
vivir	emos	We	shall	live
vivir	éis	You	will	live
vivir	án	They, you (pol.)	will	live

(b) IRREGULAR FUTURE STEMS
(*endings are normal*)

dir é (decir)
I shall say/tell
har ás (hacer)
You will do/make
podr á (poder)
He, she, you, will be able
pondr emos (poner)
We shall put
querr éis (querer)
You will want (plur.)
sabr án (saber)
They (you) will know
saldr é (salir)
I shall go out
tendr ás (tener)
You will have
vendr á (venir)
He, she, you will come
habr á { future of **hay** §36/ auxiliary for the Future Perfect §9
cabr á/án★ (caber)
It/they will fit in
valdr á/án★ (valer)
It/they will be worth
(★3rd person forms are the most common)

Many verbs which are irregular in other tenses, form the future quite regularly,
e.g. **dar**-é, **ser**-é, **ir**-é

Note that *oír* loses the accent when used as the future stem: **oir**-é, etc.

3. Usage

(a) **In reference to future time:**
    Vendremos temprano la próxima vez = We shall come early next time.
(b) **Interrogative shall...?** — use the present in Spanish.
    Shall I do it now? ¿Lo **hago** ahora?
(c) **Will** implying willingness: use *querer* (§49)
(d) To suggest **probability**: See §53

B. THE IMMEDIATE FUTURE

1. Meaning: I *am going* to finish

2. Formation: IR + A + INFINITIVE

IR	+A	+ INFINITIVE	TO GO	+ INFINITIVE
Voy	a	hablar	I am going	to speak
Vas	a	vender	You are going	to sell
Va	a	vivir	He/she ⋆ is going	to live
Vamos	a	nadar	We are going	to swim
Vais	a	ver	You are going	to see
Van	a	venir	They ⋆ are going	to come
			⋆ Also you (pol.)	

Note: estar a punto de + infinitive = { to be about to be
　　　　　　　　　　　　　　　　　　 { to be on the point of

El hombre **está a punto de** salir a la calle
= The man *is about to* go out.

§3 THE CONDITIONAL TENSE

1. Meaning: I *would* speak.

2. Formation: Future stem + Imperfect endings of -er and -ir verbs.

FUTURE STEMS	+ ENDINGS		AUXIL. VERB	
hablar	ía	I	would	speak
vender	ías	You	would	sell
vivir	ía	He/she/you	would	live
ser	íamos	We	would	be
ir	íais	You	would	go
dir	ían	They/you	would	say

Note 1: "*I should....*" and "*We should....*" are more proper in English in the first persons singular and plural.
Do not confuse this with *should = ought to*. (§32, Deber)

Note 2: Would = *used to*: use the imperfect tense.
e.g. Every morning I **would** (= *used to*) wake up at 7 o'clock.

Note 3: See § 58, **Si clauses** and conditions.

§4 THE IMPERFECT TENSE

A. MEANINGS

1. Recognition

(a) ...**WAS/WERE -ING**... (See also Progressive Tenses, §52)
While I **WAS**/we **WERE** work**ING** at the factory.

(b) ...**USED TO**... (See also §24, *soler*: to be in the habit of)
Every day I **USED TO** visit my uncle.

(c) ...**WOULD**... (when = ...**USED TO**...)
Every morning I **WOULD** visit my uncle.

(d) **THE SIMPLE PAST — DISGUISED**: I *worked*; I *visited*.
Apply this *test*: If (a), (b) or (c) can be inserted, then the Simple Past is
a **DISGUISED** Imperfect.
While I *worked* at the factory.
Test: really means **WAS** work**ING**, ∴ **Imperfect**
Every day I *visited* my uncle.
Test: really means **USED TO** (or **WOULD**) visit, ∴ Imperfect
(Remember: *would* normally indicates the **Conditional Tense**)

2. Examples of the Imperfect

	SIMPLE PAST = DISGUISED IMPERFECT
(a) Description or State **Llevaba** un pantalón azul = He *was wearing* blue trousers	he *wore*
Estábamos contentos = We *were* happy	
(b) Repetition or Habit Todos los días él **se levantaba** a las ocho, y después **tomaba** una ducha. = Every day he *used to get up* at 8 o'clock, and then he *would take* a shower.	he *got up* he *took*
(c) Continuous Background	

Estábamos comiendo... We *were eating*	cuando ellos llegaron *when they arrived*	
Mientras **estaba actuando**... While he *was acting*	se cayó al suelo *he fell down*	he *acted*
Mientras **estábamos esperando**... While we *were waiting*	nos habló *he spoke to us*	we *waited*
Continuous Background → **The Progressive Imperfect** (§52)	*Interrupted by a sudden action or event —* ↓ *The Preterite* ↓	

(d) Simultaneous, incompleted actions
Mientras yo **hablaba** él **leía** un libro.
While I *was speaking* he *was reading* a book.

	spoke...read

B. FORMATION

1. Regular — according to the infinitive ending.

— Remove the **-ar**; add the **-aba** series of endings.
— Remove the **-er** or **-ir**; add the **-ía** series of endings.

habl	(-ar)	vend	(-er)	viv	(-ir)
habl	**aba**	vend	**ía**	viv	**ía**
habl	**abas**	vend	**ías**	viv	**ías**
habl	**aba**	vend	**ía**	viv	**ía**
habl	**ábamos**	vend	**íamos**	viv	**íamos**
habl	**abais**	vend	**íais**	viv	**íais**
habl	**aban**	vend	**ían**	viv	**ían**

Note: this formation procedure applies to radical and spelling changing verbs, and to all but 3 irregular verbs:

d	**ar** → daba
est	**ar** → estaba
pens	**ar** → pensaba
lleg	**ar** → llegaba
pod	**er** → podía
volv	**er** → volvía
cog	**er** → cogía
hab	**er** → había
dec	**ir** → decía
o	**ir** → oía
ped	**ir** → pedía
argü	**ir** → argüía

2. The 3 Irregular Imperfects

ir	**ser**	**ver**
to go	*to be*	*to see*
iba	era	veía
ibas	eras	veías
iba	era	veía
íbamos	éramos	veíamos
ibais	erais	veíais
iban	eran	veían

3. The Progressive Imperfect: Imperfect of estar + Present Participle

The progressive tense describes a *continuous background condition*, indicated by **was/were** ....**ING** in English.
Estaban hablando... = They *were talking* (a continuous background during which other actions or events may take place: see also §52)

§5 THE PRETERITE TENSE: THE SIMPLE PAST

A. MEANING:

I *opened*. The auxiliary *did* is used in English in interrogative and negative forms, and for emphasis:

Did I open? I *did* not open. I *did* open.
The auxiliary *did* is never translated into Spanish.

1. Simple Narrative

Ayer, Juan **se levantó**, **salió** a la calle y después **compró** un periódico.
= Yesterday, John got up, went out, then he bought a newspaper.

Contrast the Imperfect — for **Repetition** or **Habit**.
Cada mañana, Juan *se levantaba*, *salía* a la calle, y después *compraba* un periódico.
= Every morning, John *used to get up*, *used to go out*, then he *would buy* a newspaper.

2. Completed past events and actions

Preterite for event/action	Imperfect for ⟶	
Juan **abrió** la ventana	porque *tenía* calor	: *Description or State*
María **cerró** la puerta	que *estaba* abierta	: *Description or State*
El niño **se cayó**	mientras *jugaba*	: *Continuous Background*

B. FORMATION

1. Regular

(a) -ar verbs. Remove **-ar** to form the stem, and add these endings:

habl **é**
habl **aste**
habl **ó**
habl **amos**★
habl **asteis**
habl **aron**

(b) -er and -ir verbs
Remove **-er** or **-ir**, and add these endings:

vend **í**   viv **í**
vend **iste**   viv **iste**
vend **ió**   viv **ió**
vend **imos**   viv **imos**★
vend **isteis**   viv **isteis**
vend **ieron**   viv **ieron**

(★forms identical to the Present Tense)

2. Radical changing verbs: -ir type only.

The following **STEM** changes occur in the 3rd persons:

O → U **dormir** *to sleep*		E → I			
		sentir *to feel*	**pedir** *to ask*	**reír** *to laugh*	**reñir** *to scold*
dorm í		sent í	ped í	re í	reñ í
dorm iste		sent iste	ped iste	re íste	reñ iste
dUrm ió		sInt ió	pId ió	rI ★ ó	rIñ ★ ó
dorm imos		sent imos	ped imos	re ímos	reñ imos
dorm isteis		sent isteis	ped isteis	re ísteis	reñ isteis
dUrm ieron		sInt ieron	pId ieron	rI ★ eron	rIñ ★ eron

★See **3(c)** below.

Like *dormir*   :   morir
Like *sentir*   :   advertir, consentir, divertir, herir, hervir, mentir, preferir, sugerir, transferir.
Like *pedir*   :   competir, conseguir, corregir, despedir, elegir, expedir, impedir, repetir, seguir, servir, vestir.
Like *reír*   :   sonreír, freír. **Like** *reñir*   :   teñir.

3. Spelling changing verbs

(a) Changes in the YO form before the é

-car : c → QU **buscar** *to look for*	-gar : G → GU **llegar** *to arrive*	-guar : GU → GÜ **averiguar** *to find out*	-zar : Z → C **rezar** *to pray*
busQU é	lleGU é	averiGÜ é	reC é
busc aste	lleg aste	averigu aste	rez aste
busc ó	lleg ó	averigu ó	rez ó
busc amos	lleg amos	averigu amos	rez amos
busc asteis	lleg asteis	averigu asteis	rez asteis
busc aron	lleg aron	averigu aron	rez aron

Common examples

sacar = to take out	pagar = to pay	cazar = to hunt
tocar = to touch	plegar = to fold	comenzar = to begin
cegar = to blind	rogar = to beg, pray	cruzar = to cross
colgar = to hang	apaciguar = to pacify	empezar = to begin
jugar = to play	almorzar = to lunch	forzar = to force

(b) Changes in the endings of the 3rd persons: i → Y in -aer, -eer, -oír, -uir, -oer, verbs

caer *to fall*	**leer** *to read*	**oír** *to hear*	**huir** *to flee*	**argüir** *to argue*	**roer** *to gnaw*
ca í	le í	o í	hu í	argü í	ro í
ca íste	le íste	o íste	hu iste	argü iste	ro íste
caYó	leYó	oYó	huYó	arguYó	roYó
ca ímos	le ímos	o ímos	hu imos	argü imos	ro ímos
ca ísteis	le ísteis	o ísteis	hu isteis	argü isteis	ro ísteis
caYeron	leYeron	oYeron	huYeron	arguYeron	roYeron

Like *leer*: creer = to believe.
Like *huir*: other verbs in -uir, e.g. construir, contribuir.

(c) Changes in the endings of the 3rd persons: i removed in -llir, -ñir verbs. (*Also*: R.C.V. *reñir* and *reír*, B.2 above)

bullir, *to boil*: bullí, bulliste, bull __ ó, bullimos, bullisteis, bull __ eron.
gruñir, *to grunt*: gruñí, gruñiste, gruñ __ ó, gruñimos, gruñisteis, gruñ __ eron.

4. 18 Verbs Irregular in the Preterite:

1. ANDAR *to walk*	**2. CABER** *to fit*	**3. CONDUCIR** *to drive*
anduve anduviste anduvo anduvimos anduvisteis anduvieron	cupe cupiste cupo cupimos cupisteis cupieron	conduje condujiste condujo condujimos condujisteis condujeron
4. DAR *to give*	**5. DECIR** *to say/tell*	**6. ESTAR** *to be*
di diste dio dimos disteis dieron	dije dijiste dijo dijimos dijisteis dijeron	estuve estuviste estuvo estuvimos estuvisteis estuvieron
7. HABER* *to have*	**8. HACER** *to do/make*	**9. IR** *to go*
hube hubiste hubo hubimos hubisteis hubieron	hice hiciste hizo hicimos hicisteis hicieron	fui fuiste fue fuimos fuisteis fueron
10. PODER *to be able*	**11. PONER** *to put*	**12. QUERER** *to want/love*
pude pudiste pudo pudimos pudisteis pudieron	puse pusiste puso pusimos pusisteis pusieron	quise quisiste quiso quisimos quisisteis quisieron

13. **SABER** *to know*	14. **SER** *to be*	15. **TENER** *to have/hold*
supe supiste supo supimos supisteis supieron	fui fuiste fue fuimos fuisteis fueron	tuve tuviste tuvo tuvimos tuvisteis tuvieron
16. **TRAER** *to bring*	17. **VENIR** *to come*	18. **VER** *to see*
traje trajiste trajo trajimos trajisteis trajeron	vine viniste vino vinimos vinisteis vinieron	vi viste vio vimos visteis vieron

*HABER
— the auxiliary for the Past Anterior §8
— *hubo* . . . a past tense for *hay*, §36

Also Compounds, e.g.

conducir	: introducir, producir	**tener**	: contener, detener(se) obtener, sostener
hacer	: deshacer, satisfacer		
poner	: disponer, exponer, suponer	**traer** **venir**	: distraer, substraer : convenir, intervenir

The Five Compound Tenses

§6 THE PERFECT TENSE

1. Meaning

2. Formation →

HABER in Present Tense	+ PAST PARTICIPLE (§47)	HAVE/HAS...		
yo **he**	hablado (-ar)	I	*have*	spoken
tú **has**	vendido (-er)	You	*have*	sold
él, ella } usted } **ha**	vivido (-ir)	{ He, she,	*has*	lived }
		you	*have*	lived }
nosotros, -as **hemos**	dicho ⎫	We	*have*	said
vosotros, -as **habéis**	escrito ⎬ irregular	You	*have*	written
ellos, -as; ustedes **han**	visto ⎭	They, you	*have*	seen

Note 1: The past participle is invariable in the compound tenses formed with *haber*.
(Ellas) las han vendid*o* = They have sold them.

Note 2: Reflexive pronouns and object pronouns **precede** the auxiliary *haber*:
Me *he* acostado temprano = I have gone to bed early.
Nos *has* mentido = You have lied to us.

Note 3: In Spanish, no word may stand between the auxiliary *haber* and the past participle:
Have **you** seen the film? = ¿Ha visto **usted** la película?
I have **never** eaten them = **Nunca** los he comido.

Note 4: *Have just*; *for* with time: See §37.

§7 THE PLUPERFECT (...HAD...)

The imperfect of haber: había, -ías, -ía, -íamos, -íais, -ían	+ past participle

Llegué al aeropuerto tarde, porque **había olvidado** mi reloj.
= I arrived at the airport late, because I *had forgotten* my watch.

§8 THE PAST ANTERIOR (...HAD...)

The preterite of haber: hube, -iste, -o, -imos, -isteis, -ieron	+ past participle

The **Past Anterior** replaces the **Pluperfect** when both (a) and (b) apply:

(a) *After conjunctions of time:*

cuando	= when	así que	
después (de) que	= after, when	en cuanto	} = as soon as
apenas...(cuando)	= hardly...when		

(b) *When the verb in the other clause is in the Preterite Tense:*
En cuanto **hubo comido**, se acostó.
= As soon as *he had eaten*, he went to bed.
Apenas **hube llegado**, *(cuando)* el teléfono sonó.
= Hardly *had I arrived* when the telephone rang.

Note: The Past Anterior is a formal and literary tense; in conversation
the Preterite is usually used instead:
En cuanto **comió**, se acostó.

§9 THE FUTURE PERFECT (...SHALL/WILL HAVE...)

The future of haber: habré, -ás, -á, -emos, -éis, -án	+ past participle

Lo **habrá reparado** para la próxima semana.
= He *will have repaired* it by next week.

§10 THE CONDITIONAL PERFECT
(...SHOULD/WOULD HAVE...)

The conditional of haber: habría, -ías, -ía, -íamos, -íais, -ían	+ past participle

Habría* salido, pero su coche se estropeó.
= He *would have gone out*, but his car broke down.
(* or *Hubiera salido* — see -ra forms of the **subjunctive**, §62.A.4)

Note: The Future Perfect and Conditional Perfect Tenses may suggest
probability — see §53.

Part Two — Pronouns and Adjectives

§11 SUBJECT PRONOUNS

1. Forms and meanings . . . . Corresponding verb endings				
		Present	**Imperfect**	
S			-AR	-ER/-IR
I I	= **yo** . . . . hablo		-*aba*	-*ía* ←
N You	= **tú** . . . . hablas		-abas	-ías ⌐
G He, it (masc.)	= **él** . . . . habl*a* ←		-*aba*	-*ía* ←
U she, it (fem.)	= **ella** . . . . habl*a* ← ⌐		-*aba*	-*ía* ←
L you (pol.sing.)	= **usted (Vd.)** . . . . . . habl*a* ←		-*aba*	-*ía* ←
A				
R				
P we	= **nosotros, -as** . . . . . hablamos		-ábamos	-íamos
L you (fam.plur.)	= **vosotros, -as** . . . . . habláis		-abais	-íais
U they (masc.)	= **ellos** . . . . habl*an* ←		-*aban*	-*ían* ←
R they (fem.)	= **ellas** . . . . habl*an* ← ⌐		-*aban*	-*ían* ←
A you (pol.plur.)	= **ustedes(Vds.)** . . . . habl*an* ←		-*aban*	-*ían* ←
L				

2. Basic rule

Subject pronouns are normally omitted in Spanish, especially in
conversation, since the *verb ending* indicates the subject in most cases:
   Como = *I* eat; **comprarán** = *they* will buy; **vivisteis** = *you* lived

3. When used

(a) To avoid confusion, when subject pronouns share the same verb
ending (as arrowed above), and when the person is not clear from the
context: e.g. **-aba**, and **-ía** could indicate *I, he, she, it* or *you*.
Thus: **Yo** me levantaba cuando **ella** salía de casa.
      = *I* used to get up when *she* left the house.

(b) for emphasis or to show contrast
¡**Vosotros** jugáis mientras **yo** trabajo!
= *You* play while *I* work!

4. You — four possibilities:

Tú — *familiar singular* (*tutear* = to use the *tú* form)
To a friend, to a child, to a family member, to a pet.
Vosotros — *familiar plural*
To more than one friend, child, family member, pet.
Usted/Vd. — *polite singular* (*tratar de usted* = to use the polite form)
To one respected person, child to an adult, to an unknown person
(shares the same verb ending as *él/ella*).
Ustedes/Vds. — *polite plural*
To respected persons, child to adults, to unknown persons (shares the
same verb ending as *ellos/ellas*).

5. It and **they** are normally omitted:

(a) When referring to animals and objects.
El gato está en la habitación, y __juega con el perro.
¿Dónde están los libros? — __Están en la biblioteca.

(b) When verbs are used impersonally
__Es importante = *It* is important; __Hay niebla = *It* is foggy.

(c) In phrases such as : It is I, etc.
¡Soy yo! = **It** is I! (It's me! colloquially);
¡Es ella! **It**'s her! (colloquially)
Somos nosotros quienes decidimos = **It** is we (us) who decide.

Note: **It** as a neuter subject pronoun is *ello*, referring to an idea and not
to a specific noun:
Ello no es tan importante como yo creía.
= **It** is not as important as I thought.

6. Gender

Nosotros, vosotros, ellos — masculine or *mixed* masculine/feminine
Nosotras, vosotras, ellas — feminine only.

7. Double subject and verb agreement, e.g. Ella y yo (= *we*), §61.

§12 OBJECT PRONOUNS (WEAK OR CONJUNCTIVE PRONOUNS)

1. Forms and meanings

Subject Pronoun	DIRECT OBJECT		INDIRECT OBJECT		REFLEXIVE Direct and Indirect
yo tú	**me** **te**	= me = you(fam. sing.)	**me** **te**	= to me = to you	me te
	THING lo = it(m.) la = it(f.)				
él ella usted	**le**(or *lo*) **la** { **le**(or *lo*) **la**	= him = her = you (pol. sing.)	**le** **le** **le**	= to him = to her = to you	se se se
nosotros, -as vosotros, -as	**nos** **os**	= us = you(fam. plur.)	**nos** **os**	= to us = to you	nos os
	THINGS los = them(m.) las = them(f.)				
ellos ellas ustedes	**los**(or *les*) **las** { **los**(or *les*) **las**	= them(m.) = them(f.) = you(pol. plur.)	**les** **les** **les**	= to them = to them = to you	se se se

Note 1: These alternatives are found:
lo instead of **le** for **him** and **you** (pol. sing. masc.)
les instead of **los** for **them** (masc. persons) and **you** (pol. plur. masc.)

Note 2: **Se** is used instead of **le** or **les** before another 3rd person direct object pronoun (See 5. below). Do not confuse with the reflexive **se** (See §56).

Note 3: The neuter **LO** (not shown in the above table)
(a) May represent an object understood, but not expressed in English:
Se **lo** ha dicho porque es honrado.
= He has told you (it, the facts) because he is honest.
¡Pidéselo! = Ask them (it)! ¡Ya **lo** creo! = I should think so!
(b) Saves repeating a noun or adjective:
Dice que es { enfermera / guapa } pero no **lo** es.
He says that she is { a nurse / pretty } but she is not... i.e. { a nurse / pretty }

2. Examples of usage

DIRECT OBJECT		INDIRECT OBJECT: to; and for*
(a) *me, you (fam.sing.), us*		*to me, to you(fam.sing.), to us*
Juan **me** ve.	S	**Me** da el libro.
John sees *me*.	A	= $\begin{cases} \text{He gives the book to me.} \\ \text{He gives \_\_ me the book.} \end{cases}$
	M	
Él **te** miraba.	E	**Te** mandó el regalo.
He was watching *you*.		= $\begin{cases} \text{He sent the present to you.} \\ \text{He sent \_\_ you the present.} \end{cases}$
	F	
Nos veía a menudo.	O	**Nos** escribisteis ayer.
He saw *us* often.	R	= You wrote to us yesterday.
	M	
Os invitaré también.	S	**Os** mandaré las cartas.
I will invite *you*, too.		= $\begin{cases} \text{I will send the letters to you.} \\ \text{I will send \_\_ you the letters.} \end{cases}$

DIRECT OBJECT	INDIRECT OBJECT: to; and for*
(b) *him* | *her* | *it: a thing*	*to him, to her, to it*
le | **la** | **lo**(m.), **la**(f.)	**LE** (m. or f.)
le vi = I saw *him*.	**Le** mandé el libro.
lo vendí = I sold *it*(m.)	= I sent the book **to him/to her**.
la oí = I heard *her*.	**Also:** *to you* — see (d) below.
la perdí = I lost *it*(f.)	
(c) *them:* **los**(m.), **las**(f.)	*to them:* **LES** (m. or f.)
for persons and things	**LES** di las bebidas.
Los or **las** vi = I saw *them*	= $\begin{cases} \text{I gave the drinks to them.} \\ \text{I gave \_\_ them the drinks.} \end{cases}$
(d) *you (pol.sing.):* **le**(m.), **la**(f.)	*to you (pol sing.):* **LE** (m. or f.)
Le vi (a usted)	**LE** mandé (a usted) el libro.
= I saw *you* (m.)	= $\begin{cases} \text{I sent the book to you.} \\ \text{I sent \_\_ you the book.} \end{cases}$
La oí (a usted)	
= I heard *you* (f.)	
(e) *you(pol.plur.):* **los**(m.), **las**(f.)	*to you (pol.plur.)* **LES** (m. or f.)
Los or **las** vi (a ustedes)	**Les** di (a ustedes) las bebidas.
= I saw *you* (m. or f.)	= $\begin{cases} \text{I gave the drinks to you.} \\ \text{I gave \_\_ you the drinks.} \end{cases}$

****Note 1:** *For* (somebody): translated by the indirect object pronoun, or
para + disjunctive pronoun (§13):
Te compró el regalo *or* Compró el regalo para **ti**
= He bought [*for*] *you* the present.

Note 2: a **usted**(es) is added:
(a) to specify the person (if the context does not make this clear), or
(b) for emphasis
e.g. Le vi **a usted** = I saw *you*; Le vi **a él** = I saw *him*. (See §13.2.b)

3. Position of object pronouns (including reflexive pronouns, §56)

(a) Before the verb: This is the normal position in all tenses,
whether affirmative, negative or interrogative;
Lo vi en el museo = I saw it in the museum.
No **la** conozco = I do not know her.
¿**Se** han levantado? = Have they got up? (*Reflexive*)

(b) Attached to the end of:
(i) Infinitives
Tengo que abrir**lo** = I must open it.
Estoy encantado de ver**te** = I am pleased to see you.
Quieren acostar**se** = They want to go to bed. (*Reflexive*)

(ii) Present Participles
Estoy reparándo**los** = I am repairing them.
Mientras estaba afeitándo**me**... = While I was shaving...(*Reflexive*)

Note: When the main verb governs the infinitive or present participle,
there is a choice of position:
BEFORE ... *or* ... ATTACHED

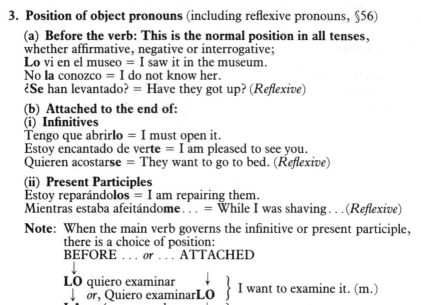

LO quiero examinar   ↓   } I want to examine it. (m.)
  ↓ *or*, Quiero examinar**LO** }
LA está preparando   ↓   } He is preparing it. (f.)
    or, Está preparándo**LA** }

(iii) The affirmative imperative (See §38 for full details)

¡Cóme**lo**!   = Eat it!
¡Vénda**la** usted! = Sell it!

> Negative: Pronouns precede as normal
> ¡No **lo** comas!   = Don't eat it!
> ¡No **la** venda usted! = Don't sell it!

4. Order of object pronouns when two occur

Indirect precedes direct whether:

(a) Before the verb:
Juan **te** *la* manda = John sends it to you.
Los niños **nos** *las* han dado = The children have given them to us.

or **(b) Attached to the end:**
Va a mandár**telo** = He is going to send it to you.
Pása**melos** = Pass them to me.

5. The indirect *le* and *les* become **SE**, if followed by another third person
pronoun:

not **le** { **SE** lo mandé (a él/a ella) = I sent it *to him/to her*.
        { Voy a dár**SE**los (a usted) = I am going to give them *to you*.
not **les** { **SE** las mandas (a ellos/a ellas) = You send them *to them*.
        { Quiero mandár**SE**la (a ustedes) = I want to send it *to you*.
        (**a** + strong pronoun is often added to specify the person.)
Note: In 3, 4 & 5 above the accent (´) is added to maintain stress
– See §21.

6. If the **object★** precedes the verb, "**sum up**" in object pronoun form:

★**Direct:**	*Ese coche*	**LO**	vi ayer = I saw that car yesterday.
★**Indirect:**	*Al jefe*	**LE**	expliqué la razón = I explained the reason to the boss.
Note also for emphasis:		**LES**	he dado regalos *a sus hijos.*

§13 DISJUNCTIVE PRONOUNS (STRONG OR PREPOSITIONAL PRONOUNS)

1. Forms and meanings

DISJUNCTIVE PRONOUNS			Corresponding Subject Pronouns
Non-reflexive		**Reflexive**	
mí = me	**mí**	= myself	yo
ti (no ´) = you	**ti** (no ´)	= yourself	tú
él = him, it (m.)	**sí**	= himself	él
ella = her, it (f.)	**sí**	= herself	ella
usted = you	**sí**	= yourself	usted
nosotros, -as = us	**nosotros, -as**	= ourselves	nosotros, -as
vosotros, -as = you	**vosotros, -as**	= yourselves	vosotros, -as
ellos = them	**sí**	= themselves	ellos
ellas = them	**sí**	= themselves	ellas
ustedes = you	**sí**	= yourselves	ustedes
Also: **ello** = it (idea)			
Same forms as subject pronouns, except **mí** *&* **ti**	**sí** *is used for all third person forms*		

Note: Con combines + *mí, ti* and *sí*: con**MIGO**, con**TIGO** and con**SIGO**.

2. Usage: Disjunctive Pronouns are used after prepositions, e.g.

Estaba de pie **delante de ti** = He was standing in front of you.
Quiero ir **contigo** = I want to go with you.

(a)	**Non-reflexive** . . . . . . *and* . . . **Reflexive Disjunctives** *(Same person as the subject)*	
	Los compró **para él.** = He bought them for him. (i.e. *somebody else*)	Los compró **para sí.** He / She / You (pol.) bought them for { himself / herself / yourself
	Yo salía **con ella** = I went out with her	Lo trajo **consigo** He / She / You (pol.) brought it with { him / her / you [self / self / rself]

(b) a + disjunctive pronouns

(i) Used to specify (or to emphasise) the person when using:
— *Indirect object pronouns*
Le di (*a él, a ella, a usted*) el dinero.
= I gave to him, to her, to you (pol. sing.) the money.
Les di (*a ellos, a ellas, a ustedes*) el dinero.
= I gave to them, to you (pol. plur.) the money.
Se lo di (*a él, a ella, a usted, a ellos, a ellas, a ustedes*)
= I gave it to him, to her, to you (pol. sing), to them, to you (pol. plur.)
— *Direct object pronouns:* Personal **a** (§48) + disjunctive pronoun
le vi (*a él, a usted*)   = I saw him; you (pol. masc. sing.)
la vi (*a ella, a usted*)   = I saw her; you (pol. fem. sing.)
los vi (*a ellos, a ustedes*) = I saw them(m.); you (pol. masc. plur.)
las vi (*a ellas, a ustedes*) = I saw them(f.); you (pol. fem. plur.)

(ii) used for emphasis
A nosotros nos gusta el clima = *We* like the climate.

(iii) used when the verb is not expressed
¿A quién has vendido el reloj? — **A él.**
To whom have you sold the watch? To him (. . . have I sold the watch.)

(iv) used instead of *an indirect object pronoun* if **me**, **te**, **nos** or **os** already stand as **direct object pronoun:**

| **Te** | recomendaré | *a ellos* | = I will recommend **you** *to them.* |
| **Me** | recomendó | *a él* | = He recommended **me** *to him.* |

(c) After prepositions governed by verbs (See §51)
¿Qué piensas **de ella**?   = What do you think (= opinion) of her?
Estoy pensando **en él**   = I am thinking of him.
Soñaba **con ello**   = I was dreaming of it (an idea, not a
                                    specific noun).
Se preocupa **de mí**   = He is worrying about me.
Me estoy cansando **de ellos**   = I am getting tired of them.

(d) After verbs of motion
Me acerqué **a él** = I approached him.

(e) *Yo* and *tú* are used instead of *mí* and *ti* after these prepositions:

entre = between	como = like	excepto
según = according to	incluso = including	salvo ⎫ = except
		menos ⎭

e.g. como **tú** = like you   incluso **yo** = including me
Entre **tú** y **yo** vamos a resolver el problema
= Between *you* and *me* we are going to solve the problem.

(f) Add *mismo*, **-a, -os, -as** for extra emphasis:
Te lo enseñé **a ti mismo** = I showed it **to you yourself.**
La niña escribió la carta **por sí misma.**
= The child wrote the letter *by herself.*

Note: *Mismo* may also emphasise subject pronouns:
Yo *mismo* lo he leído = I *myself* have read it.

§14 DEMONSTRATIVE ADJECTIVES

1. Forms and meanings	M.S.	M.Pl.	F.S	F.Pl.
(a) This/these: *"here"*, *near speaker*	este	estos	esta	estas
(b) That/those: *"there"*, *near listener*	ese	esos	esa	esas
(c) That/those: *"over there"*, *away from speaker and listener*	aquel	aquellos	aquella	aquellas

These adjectives **precede** the noun, and they **agree** in gender and number with it.

2. Examples:

Esta casa es vieja.	= **This** house (*here*) is old.
Esa tienda de enfrente es moderna.	= **That** house (*there*) opposite is modern.
¿Ves **aquella** casita en el valle?	= Do you see **that** cottage (*down there*) in the valley?

Note 1: The demonstrative adjective is repeated before each noun:
Este lápiz y **esta** regla son baratos.
= This pencil and __ ruler are cheap.

Note 2: Examples relating to time:
En **este** momento = now   **Esta** noche = tonight
En **aquel** tiempo = then, at that time

§15 DEMONSTRATIVE PRONOUNS

1. Forms and meanings	M.S.	M.Pl.	F.S	F.Pl.
(a) This one/these *"here"*	éste	éstos	ésta	éstas
(b) That one/those *"there"*	ése	ésos	ésa	ésas
(c) That one/those *"over there"*	aquél	aquéllos	aquélla	aquéllas

These pronouns **replace** the noun, and take the same *gender* and *number* as the noun replaced.

— The **accent** (´) is added to these pronouns to distinguish them from the *Demonstrative Adjectives* (§14):
esta casa = this house; **ésta** = this one.
Remember also estar: él está (present tense); ¡Estáte quieto! (imperative)

(d) Neuter forms:

esto	= *this*	These are **invariable**, and refer to a previous idea, state, feeling, etc.
eso **aquello** }	= *that*	These forms do **not** have an accent.

2. Usage

(a) éste, ése, aquél
Este libro es útil, pero **ése** no.
= *This* book is useful, but not *that one.*
¿En qué casa vivía usted? — En **aquélla.**
= In which house were you living? — In *that one* (over there).

(b) Former and latter { aquél = former } : Agreement with the noun
{ éste = latter } referred to.

Veo una **maleta** y un *bolso*; **aquélla** es azul, *éste* es negro.
└─the former────────────┘ └────────────the latter┘

(c) esto, eso, aquello — neuter forms not referring to a specific noun
¡**Esto** es estupendo! = This is marvellous!
¡**Eso** es! = That's it!
Ahora no pienso nunca en **aquello** = I never think about that now.

(d) Definite article used as a demonstrative pronoun before *DE* and *QUE*
(i) *the one(s) of, that/those of, (John)'s:* **el, la, los, las** + **DE:**
Mis *botas* son negras; *las de* Juan son marrones.
└────────────────┘ (John's/those of John)

(ii) *the one(s), those who/which:* **el, la, los, las** + **QUE** and relative
clause (See also §18.D):
Vi **las que** compró = I saw *the ones which* he bought.
Los que (or quienes) se esfuerzan tendrán éxito
= *Those who* strive hard will succeed.

§16 POSSESSIVE ADJECTIVES

1. The more common SHORT forms:
— They precede the noun, and agree with that noun and not with the possessor.
— They all agree in number; **nuestro/s** and **vuestro/s** also agree in gender.

	Singular		Plural		Corresponding Subject Pronouns
my	mi		mis		yo
your (fam. sing.)	tu		tus		tú
his, her, its; your (pol. sing.)	su	**FEM:**	sus	**FEM:**	él, ella; Vd.
our	nuestro	-a	nuestros	-as	nosotros, -as
your (fam. plur.)	vuestro	-a	vuestros	-as	vosotros, -as
their; your (pol. plur.)	su		sus		ellos, ellas, Vds.

Examples:
Vendí **mis** libros = I (singular) sold *my* books (plural).
¿Olvidaste **tus** libros? = Did you (singular) forget *your* books (plural)?
¡Vosotras chicas debéis respetar a **vuestro** profesor!
= You girls (fem. plur.) must respect *your* teacher (masc. sing.)!

Note 1: Su and **sus** can mean: *his, her, its, their; your* (pol. sing./plur.)
       If the context does not make the possessor clear:
  (i) Add **de él, de ella, de ellos, de ellas** or **de usted(es)** after the noun.
  (ii) Change *su* → **el/la**, and *sus* → **los/las**.
La eperanza *de ellos* = Their hope. *La* corbata *de él* = His tie.
Las (or sus★) esperanzas *de usted(es)* = Your hopes.
(★*su/sus* may be retained in conjunction with usted(es))

Note 2: Possessive adjectives are normally repeated in Spanish:
    Tu magnetófono y **tus** casetes están en el salón
    Your tape recorder and __ cassettes are in the lounge.

2. The less common LONG forms
They follow the noun and agree with it in gender and number ⟶

mío	= of mine, my	**nuestro**	= of ours, our	**MS:**	-o
tuyo	= of yours, your	**vuestro**	= of yours, your	**FS:**	-a
suyo	= (of) his, of hers, her; of yours, your	**suyo**	= { of theirs, their / of yours, your	**MPl:**	-os
				FPl:	-as

Uses
(a) *To translate* **of mine, of yours, of hers,** etc.
    un amigo **vuestro** = a friend of yours
(b) *For emphasis*
    Prefiere las pinturas **tuyas.** = He prefers *your* paintings.
(c) *Personal address and exclamations*
    Muy señor **mío,**... = Dear Sir,... (in letters)
    ¡Escríbeme, hijo **mío**! = Write to me, my (dear) son!
Note: If the meaning of **suyo, -a, -os, -as** is not clear, use *de él, de usted*
    (etc.) instead
    Era la mujer [suya] { *de él* = It was **his** wife. / *de usted* = It was **your** wife.

§17 POSSESSIVE PRONOUNS

1. Formation and meanings
— Definite article + LONG FORM possessive adjective.

	M.S.	F.S.	M.Pl.	F.Pl.
mine	el mío	la mía	los míos	las mías
yours	el tuyo	la tuya	los tuyos	las tuyas
his/hers; yours	el suyo	la suya	los suyos	las suyas
ours	el nuestro	la nuestra	los nuestros	las nuestras
yours	el vuestro	la vuestra	los vuestros	las vuestras
theirs; yours	el suyo	la suya	los suyos	las suyas

2. Usage: Possessive Pronouns agree with the noun they replace:

Nuestra casa está detrás de **la tuya** = Our house is behind *yours*.
Compré unas tazas...Pedro rompió **las nuestras** = ...Peter broke *ours*.

3. The meaning of **el suyo** (etc.) may not be clear from the context.

In the example below, ambiguity is removed by replacing **las suyas** by the
definite article + de + appropriate personal pronoun:

Mis manos son más grandes que [las suyas]
= My hands are bigger than...

$$\begin{cases} las\ de\ él & = his \\ las\ de\ ella & = hers \\ las\ de\ ellos/as & = theirs \\ las\ de\ usted(es) & = yours \end{cases}$$

4. The possessive pronoun after ser:

(a) **The definite article is normally omitted**, and the pronoun functions
adjectively to indicate possession:
Aquellos campos son **míos** = Those fields are *mine*.

(b) **The article is retained** to imply contrast or to show emphasis:
Aquellos campos son *los* **míos**, pero éstos son *los* **suyos** (*or* de él).
= Those fields are *mine*, but those are *his*.

§18 RELATIVE PRONOUNS

These pronouns **refer back** to previously mentioned nouns.

A. THE SIMPLE SUBJECT OR OBJECT, POSSESSIVE AND NEUTER RELATIVES

1. QUE: Subject or Object = *who, whom, which* (that).

— Refers to *persons or things*, and is the most common relative pronoun. It
is invariable.

	SUBJECT	OBJECT
Persons	La señora **que** es anciana = The lady *who* is elderly	Las señoras **que** admiro = The ladies (*whom* ★) I admire
Things	Los coches **que** son azules = The cars *which* are blue	El coche **que** compré = The car (*which* ★) I bought

★ **Note 1:** The relative pronoun may be omitted in English, but never in Spanish.

Note 2: personal *a* + **quien(es)** may translate the direct object *whom*, but **que** is more normal: Las señoras **que** (a quienes) admiro.

2. Cuyo -a, -os, -as: possessive = whose $\begin{cases} \text{of whom for persons} \\ \text{of which for things} \end{cases}$

This relative adjective precedes the noun with which it agrees.
El niño **cuya** hermana estaba enferma = The child *whose* sister was ill.
El coche **cuyos** faros no funcionan = The car *whose* headlamps do not work.

Note: *Whose* in questions is *¿de quién(es)?* (§19)

3. Lo cual or lo que = which, what (= that which).

Neuter and invariable, referring to a previous idea or action, not to a specific noun.
Lo que me dijiste no es verdad = *What* (= *that which*) you told me is not true.
Abrió la ventana, **lo cual** me molestó = He opened the window, *which* annoyed me.

B. RELATIVE PRONOUNS AFTER PREPOSITIONS

1. Quien, quienes = whom (*for persons only*)

— *Singular and plural forms only, with no distinction for gender*
El cliente **a quien** vendí la corbata
= The customer (whom) I sold the tie *to*.★
Las amigas **con quienes** juego = The friends (*whom*) I play *with*.★

★**Note:** In English, the preposition may be separated from the relative pronoun (if expressed). In Spanish they must stand together.

2. El cual or el que series = which (for things)	M.S.	F.S.	M.Pl.	F.Pl.
	el cual el que	la cual la que	los cuales los que	las cuales las que

— *These pronouns agree in gender and number with the noun referred to.*

La tapia **contra** **(la cual)** / **(la que)** yo apoyé mi bicicleta.

= The wall against which I leaned my bicycle.

El camión **debajo** **(del cual)** / **(del que)** se escondía.

= The lorry beneath which he was hiding.

Note 1: The compound preposition **debajo de** combines with **el**. (§25)

Note 2: After the prepositions *a*, *de*, *con*, *en*, **QUE** alone
            may be used instead of the **el cual/el que** series:

La pala **con que** cavaba = The spade (which) he was digging with.
La oficina **en que** (or *donde**) trabajo = The office in which (where)
                                     I work.
El tema **de que** escribía = The subject (which) he was writing about.
La fortuna **a que** aspira = The fortune to which he aspires.
(*Donde is a relative adverb in this situation.)

C. CIRCUMSTANCES WITH A CHOICE OF RELATIVE PRONOUNS

1. In non-restrictive clauses que may be replaced by the
el cual/el que series; or by **quien(es)**.
(Non-restrictive clauses are normally enclosed within commas, and provide
less important information than the main clause.)

    (a) As subject

                              (la cual)

La hija de Pedro, [que]   **(la que)**   vive en España, viene hoy.

                              (quien)

= Peter's daughter, who lives in Spain, is coming today.

Note: The feminine **la cual/la que** refers to *la hija*, thus clarifying which
       person lives in Spain. (See also 2. below)

    (b) As object

                         ⌐——note the personal **a** (§48)

                        (al cual)

Este hombre, [que]   **(al que)**   admiramos mucho, ha sido promovido.

                    (a quien)

= This man, whom we admire greatly, has been promoted.

2. To avoid ambiguity or to emphasise, the **el cual/el que** series may be
   used instead of **que**:

    (a) for persons

La mujer de mi jefe [que]   { (i) el cual/el que }   llegó el lunes.
                           { (ii) la cual/la que }

(i) The wife of my **boss who** arrived on Monday.

(ii) My boss's **wife who** arrived on Monday.

(b) for things

¿Dónde está la llave del maletín [que] $\left\{\begin{array}{l}\text{(i) el cual/el que}\\ \text{(ii) la cual/la que}\end{array}\right\}$ hallaste?

(i) Where is the key of the **brief-case which** you found?

(ii) Where is the brief-case **key which** you found?

D. SPECIAL USES

1. He who, those who, the one(s) who/which:
El que series for persons or things; **quien(es)** for persons only.
Los que (or quienes) se levantan temprano cogen el autobús.
= *Those who* get up early catch the bus.
¿Las cartas? — He hallado **las que** él perdió ayer.
= The letters? — I found *the ones which* he lost yesterday.

2. It is I, he, she, etc. after **ser: el que** series or **quien(es)**

Soy yo el que (or quien) lo hallé.
= It is I (me, colloquially) who found it.

3. All + relative pronoun

(a) Referring to a previous noun: todos los que/todas las que
Todas las que eran interesantes. (e.g. las historias)
= All the ones (those) which were interesting.

(b) Referring to a previous idea or action: $\left\{\begin{array}{l}\text{todo lo que}\\ \text{or cuanto}\end{array}\right\}$ (invariable)
Todo lo que (or cuanto) él oía, creía.
= All that/everything he heard he would believe.

§19 INTERROGATIVE PRONOUNS AND ADJECTIVES
They all carry an accent (´)

1. ¿Quién(es)? = who, whom — *referring to persons only*.

Subject: ¿**Quién** habla? = Who is speaking?
Object: ¿*A* **quién** buscas? = Whom are you looking for?
          —Personal *a* — see §48.
After a preposition: ¿**Detrás de quién** estabas parado?
          = Behind whom were you standing?
Indirect questions: Me preguntaba **quién** telefoneó ayer.
          = I wondered who telephoned yesterday.

2. ¿De quién(es)? = Whose (Cuyo, §18.A.2, never introduces a question).

¿**De quién** es el coche? = Whose is the car?
(*or*, ¿*A* **quién** pertenece el coche?)

3. ¿Qué? = What? — an invariable pronoun referring to *things* as subject, object or after a preposition.

¿**Qué** pasa? = What is happening?
¿**Qué** compró? = What did he buy?
¿Con **qué** lo abrió? = What did he open it with?

Note: ¿**Qué?** + **ser** is used in simple question forms to elicit a definition:
¿**Qué** es esto? — Es una taza rota.
What is this? — It is a broken cup.

4. ¿Qué? = Which/what + noun — an invariable adjective referring to persons or things.

¿**Qué** revistas lee usted? = Which magazines do you read?
¿**Qué** muchacho ganó? = Which boy won?

5. ¿Cuál(es)? — pronoun which may refer to persons or things.

(a) = which one(s) — more specific than the adjective ¿**qué?** + noun (see 4. above), and implies choice:
¿**Cuál de** las revistas lee usted?
= Which (one) of the magazines do you read?

¿**Cuáles** (de mis amigos) han llegado?
= Which (of my friends) have arrived?

(b) = **What/which** before the verb *ser* is normally translated by ¿**cuál(es)?**
¿**Cuáles** eran tus aspiraciones? = What were your aspirations?
¿**Cuál** es el buen camino? = Which/what is the right way?

Exception: simple questions demanding a definition — see 3 above.

6. ¿Cuánto, -a, -os, -as? = How much (many)? — pronoun and adjective

¿**Cuánto** vale? = How much is it?
¿**Cuántas** flores tienes? = How many flowers have you got?

7. Interrogative adverbs

¿(A)dónde? = Where (to)?
¿Cuándo? = When?
¿Cómo? = How?

¿**Por qué?** = Why? — *reason*
¿**Para qué?** = Why? — *purpose*
(See §45)

¿Adónde vas? = Where are you going (to)?
¿Cómo se llama usted? = What's your name?

8. Exclamatives and other idioms

¡**Qué** guapa es ella! = How pretty she is!
¡**Qué** ruido! = What a noise!
¡**Qué** libro tan (*or* más) útil! = What a useful book!
¡**Cuánto** come este chico! = How much this lad eats!
¡**Cómo** me gusta el queso! = How I like cheese!
¿**Qué** tal? = How are you?
¿**Cómo?** or ¿**Qué?** (. . .¿ha dicho usted?) = What? i.e. Pardon?

§20 INDEFINITE ADJECTIVES AND PRONOUNS

1. Some or any — adjective
= a few, a little.

M.S.	F.S.	M.Pl.	F.Pl.
algún*	alguna	algunos unos	algunas unas

(*See §22, *shortened forms*)

Tenemos **algún** dinero = We have some (a little) money
¿Hallaste **algunas/unas** monedas?
= Did you find any (a few) coins?
Unos médicos y **unas** enfermeras fueron a ayudarles.
= Some doctors and __ nurses went to help them. (Note the repetition)

Note 1: The word for some or any is often omitted in Spanish, as occurs in
English:
Están cogiendo __ fresas = They are gathering (some) strawberries.

Note 2: *alguno* functions *negatively* after the noun — see §42.

2. A few ... few.

a few, a little — i.e. some	few, little, i.e. not many/much
Emplea **unos pocos** * obreros. He employs a few workers. Tengo **un poco de** tabaco. I have some tobacco. (*Also: unos cuantos/unas cuantas)	Emplea **pocos** obreros. He employs few workers. Tengo **poco** tabaco. I have not much tobacco.

3. Some/any (one-s); a few (pronoun): *Alguno, -a, -os, -as*
Hallé las sillas — **algunas** están rotas.
= I found the chairs — some/a few are broken.
¿He hablado con **alguno** de ustedes?
= Have I spoken with (any) one of you?

4. Somebody, anybody: *alguien* — invariable pronoun.
Alguien se acerca = Somebody is approaching.
¿He olvidado *a* **alguien**? = Have I forgotten anybody?
           ⌐——personal *a*, §48.

5. Something/anything: *algo* — invariable pronoun

Tiene **algo** en su bolsillo = He has something in his pocket.
¿**Algo** más? = Anything more?
Note: *algo* + adjective means rather:
Mi amigo está *algo* triste hoy = My friend is *rather* sad today.

6. All and every

(a) Todo: el/la/los/las + noun = all (the); the whole; each/every.

M.S.	Todo el edificio	= the whole building/all the building
M.Pl.	Todos los edificios	= all the buildings/every★ building
F.S.	Toda la noche	= all night (long)
F.Pl.	Todas las noches	= every★ night

★*or:* cada edificio
cada noche

(b)

Cada = each/every (Invariable adjective)	**Cada** (cual) (uno-a) = each/every one (Pronoun)
Felicitó a **cada** alumno. = He congratulated every pupil	**Cada** (cual) compra su propio (uno-a) libro. = Everyone buys his own book.
Fracasa **cada** vez. = He fails every time.	**Cada una** de estas reglas . . . (F.S.) = Every one of these rules . . .

(c) Todo, -a + singular noun = every (i.e., allowing for no exceptions).
Todo soldado conoce su deber.
= Each and every soldier knows his duty.

(d) Todos, -as = all (i.e. everybody)
Todos vienen temprano = Everybody comes early.
(But: Todo el mundo **viene** temprano − singular verb, see also §61)
Todas vosotras (fem. plur.) habéis ganado = You have all won.

(e) Todo = **all** (i.e., everything, all of it)
Todo está perdido = All is lost.
Lo he olvidado **todo**. (Insert lo when todo is the object)

(f) All + relative pronoun — see §18.D.3.

7. List of common indefinite adjectives: §22.C.

Part Three — Points Alphabetically

§21 ACCENTUATION AND ALPHABET

A. ACCENTUATION

1. **The normal rules of stress are:**

    (a) **Stress on the PENULTIMATE syllable** — *words ending in* . . .

a VOWEL	-N	or -S
la limonada, compro,	andan	los zapatos

    (b) **Stress on the LAST syllable** — *words ending in* . . .

a CONSONANT (except -n or -s):
el papel, el doctor, andaluz, la ciudad

    (c) **Vowel combinations**
    — *strong vowels:* **a, e, o** — they are pronounced separately,
    and stressed on the **PENULTIMATE** syllable: veo, leen, ideas
    or stressed on the LAST syllable . . . . :real, ideal
    — *weak vowels:* **i, u** — stress the second:
    fuimos, ruido; viuda
    — *Strong and weak mixed:* stress the strong:
    pienso, el guante (*but:* el país, mío, tío, see 2. below)

2. **The accent (′) is used:**

    (a) **when the normal rules of stress are not followed:**

máquina	*not* maquina	;	compró	*not* compro
el andén	*not* anden	;	los demás	*not* demas
el árbol	*not* arbol	;	el lápiz	*not* lapiz

(b) To differentiate between words of the same spelling:

aun	= even	aún	= yet, still
de	= of, from, about	dé	= pres. subj. of dar
el	= the	él	= he
mas	= but	más	= more
mi	= my	mí	= me
se	= (reflexive pronoun (§56) (special ind. obj. pron. (§12)	sé	= I know (saber); Be! (ser)
si	= if	sí	= yes; himself, etc. (§13)
solo	= alone	sólo	= only (§42)
te	= (reflexive pronoun (you, object pronoun	té	= tea
tu	= your	tú	= you (fam. sing.)
demonstrative adjectives: este, ese, aquel, etc. (§14)		**demonstrative pronouns:** éste, ése, aquél, etc. (§15)	
relatives, conjunctions, adverbs: quien, como, cuando		**interrogatives, exclamatives:** ¿quién? ¡cómo! ¿cuándo?	

(c) To maintain the original stress when object pronouns are attached to:

Present participles: yo estaba leyéndolo = I was reading it.
Imperative/commands: ¡Dámelo! = Give it to me!
Infinitive + two pronouns:
Quiero mandárselos = I want to send them to him.
    (*but:* Quiero mandarlos a Juan — no accent).

Note: See also §22, *Adjectives* and §43, *plural of nouns.*

B. THE ALPHABET

1. Extra letters

ch — pronounced as in English: la chica = girl
ñ — pronounced ny as in onion: cañón = canyon
ll — pronounced lli as in million: un millón; la calle.

Note the order of **ch, ñ,** *and* **ll** *in Spanish dictionaries:*

océano	anadeja	valiente
ocurrir	anuncio	valva
ocho	añadir	valle

2. Double letters

cc — each c is pronounced separately: lec/ción
nn — (rare) — separate pronunciation: in/nato — inborn
rr — more trilled than the single r: pero; perro

Spanish often uses a singular letter where the English equivalent has double letters:
ocupar, pasar, inteligente, oficina, ilegible.

Note on the diaeresis (¨)
u is silent in these formations: **gu** + **e** and **gu** + **i**
e.g. llegué = I arrived.   distinguimos = we distinguish(ed)
However, in **gü** + **e**, and **gü** + **i**, the **ü** is pronounced.
e.g. apacigüé = I pacified.   argüimos = we argue(d).

3. Capital letters

Capital letters	**small initial letters**
Countries	Nationality and language, §29
Proper names: **J**uan **L**ópez	Days and months, §31
Abbreviated titles: **Sr.** Ruiz	Titles: (el) **s**eñor Ruiz, §25
First letter of a book title:	
Punto por punto	

§22 ADJECTIVES

A. AGREEMENT

TYPES OF ADJECTIVES	FEMININE FORMS		PLURAL FORMS		
	1. Ending in -A		Add **-S** to singular (vowel) Add **-ES** to singular (consonant)		
	MASCULINE	FEMININE	MASCULINE	FEMININE	MEANINGS
Final -O: **Change to A**	rojo ⟶	rojA	rojoS	rojaS	red
ADD -A to: *Adjectives of Nationality and Region*	español ⟶ inglés ⟶ catalán ⟶ andaluz ⟶	españolA inglesA catalanA andaluzA	españolES inglesES catalanES andalucES	españolaS inglesaS catalanaS andaluzaS	Spanish English Catalan Andalusian
ADD -A to: *final -an,* *-on, -in, -or★*	glotón ⟶ amador ⟶	glotonA amadorA	glotonES amadorES	glotonaS amadoraS	greedy loving
Final -E: No change	**2. SHARED SINGULAR** **MASC ↔ FEM** libre		**SHARED PLURAL** **MASC ↔ FEM** libreS	free	
Final consonant: No change	azul cortés joven feroz		azulES cortesES jóvenES ferocES	blue polite young ferocious	

*Note 1: Irregular comparatives have shared singular and shared plural forms:
mejor, mejor; mejores, mejores.
Also: menor, mayor, peor, inferior, superior, exterior, interior, posterior,
anterior, ulterior.

Note 2: Some adjectives end in **-a** in the masculine:
pesimista, -a; -as, -as...pessimistic
belga, -a, -as, -as...Belgian.

Note 3: *Accent removed:* inglesa, catalana, glotona, (etc.); corteses.
Accent added: jóvenes.

Note 4: **Z → C** before **e** or **i**, Hence: andaluCes, feroCes.

Note 5: Adjectives qualifying nouns of mixed gender — use the masculine plural:
Las montañas y los campos hermosos.

B. SHORTENED FORMS (APOCOPATED)

1. Losing -o: before masculine and singular nouns:

			Examples
a, one	uno	un (See §44)	
good	bueno	buen	Un **buen** libro = a good book
bad	malo	mal	El **primer** año = the first year
first	primero	primer	¿Tienes **algún** queso?
third	tercero	tercer	*But:*
some, any	alguno	algún	una *buena* idea (feminine)
no, not any	ninguno	ningún	los *primeros* chicos (plural)

2. Santo → San (= Saint): before masculine proper nouns.

San Juan
San Sebastián   *But:* { *Santo* Domingo, *Santo* Tomás (before Do- and To-);
{ *Santa* María (feminine).

3. Grande → gran: before any singular noun

un **gran** ministro   *but:* un edificio *grande* ⎫
= a great minister   = a big building   ⎬ *after the noun*
La **Gran** Bretaña   *but:* Río *Grande*   ⎭

4. Ciento → cien: before nouns and mil (See also §44)

cien días = a hundred days. **Cien** mil = 100,000.

5. Cual(es)quiera: loses the -a before a noun (See also §62.B.7)

cualquier niño = any child

C. POSITION OF ADJECTIVES

1. AFTER the noun: the normal position

Una camisa **azul**.   La gramática **española**.

2. BEFORE the noun

(a) Common indefinite adjectives

alguno	= some	cual(es)quiera	= any	poco/s	= little/few
ninguno	= no	demasiado	= too much	semejante	= such
ambos	= both	lo, los, las demás (inv.) }	= the rest, remaining	tal	= such (a)
bastante	= enough	mucho	= a lot of	tanto	= as much
cada (inv.)	= each	otro	= (an)other	todo	= every

(b) Short common adjectives often stand before the noun:
bueno, malo, grande, hermoso, pequeño, joven, viejo, próximo, primero (and other ordinals).

Note: *an adverb + adjective combination* follows the noun:
un viejo coche *but* un coche *muy viejo*.

(c) Adjectives reinforcing the essential quality of the noun often precede:
La **altísima** montaña. El **eminente** profesor.
Las **doradas** praderas = The golden meadows.

3. Two adjectives

(a) One may precede (either in accordance with the above rules, or because it is the more significant).
La pequeña taza roja = The little red cup.
La inmensa montaña imponente = The huge imposing mountain.

(b) Both may follow *linked with* y (quite normal)
Un regalo *inútil y caro* = A useless and expensive present.

(c) Both may precede, *linked with* y (rather formal)
El eminente y erudito profesor = The eminent and learned professor.

4. Changed meaning by changed position

	BEFORE	*AFTER*
grande	un **gran** general = a great general	un camión *grande* = a big lorry
pobre	¡La **pobre** mujer! = the poor (pitiable) woman!	una mujer *pobre* = a poor (penniless) woman
nuevo	un **nuevo** esfuerzo = a new (another) attempt	un coche *nuevo* = a (brand) new car
varios	**varios** discos = several records	discos *varios* = different records
mismo	la **misma** idea = the same/very idea	la idea *misma* . . . . = the idea itself . . .
antiguo	un **antiguo** soldado a former soldier	la catedral *antigua* = the ancient cathedral

§23 ADVERBS

1. Formation: Add **-MENTE** (= *-LY*) to the **feminine adjective** (§22)

Masculine	Feminine	Adverb	Meaning
rápido ⟶	**rápida** ⟶	rápida*mente*	= quick*ly*
fácil ⟵⟶	**fácil** ⟶	fácil*mente*	= easi*ly*
posible ⟵⟶	**posible** ⟶	posible*mente*	= possib*ly*

Note 1: *Irregular adverbs:*
bueno → bien (well); malo → mal (badly);
poco and mucho have a form identical to the M.S. adjective.

Note 2: *Not all adverbs end in -mente*, e.g. despacio (slowly)
Others are formed **con** + noun: **con** simpatía *or*
simpática*mente*.

2. Position of adverbs: never between **haber** and the past participle, and
not usually between the subject and the verb:

I have *accidentally* broken it = *Por descuido* lo he ⎍ roto.

John *frequently* complains = Juan ⎍ se queja *con frecuencia*
(frecuentemente).

3. Two adverbs together: remove *-mente* from the first adverb:

Habla sincera [mente] y respetuosa*mente* . . . sincerely and respectfully.

4. Certain adjectives may be used adverbially (note agreement):

Bajaron la calle, ruidos**os** y agresiv**os** . . . noisily and aggressively.

5. Recientemente shortens to *recién* before a past participle:
el *recién* nacido = the newly born.

§24 AGAIN AND USUALLY

A. AGAIN

1. VOLVER A + **infinitive** (*volver* = to return/turn; *volverse* = to turn round)

Volvieron a probarlo = They tried it again.
Vuelve a llover   = It is raining again.

2. De nuevo, otra vez = again, once more.

Lo hará **de nuevo/otra vez** = He will do it again.

B. USUALLY

SOLER + infinitive (present and imperfect only)
Suele nevar en invierno = It usually snows in winter.
Solíamos jugar después de la cena = We were *accustomed to playing/used to play* after dinner.
(**Also:** Jugábamos después de la cena.)

§25 ARTICLES

A. TYPES

	M.S.	F.S.	M.Pl.	F.Pl.
1. **Definite:** *the* →	EL	LA	LOS	LAS
2. **Indefinite:** *a, an* →	UNO/UN	UNA	UNOS	UNAS
3. **The neuter LO**	(See §22)		(See §20, Some)	

B. SPECIAL FORMS AND USES

1. Combinations
a + *el* = **AL:** *to the*
Di el juguete **AL** chico (but: **a la** chica/**a los** chicos/**a las** chicas).
de + *el* = **DEL:** *of the* indicating possession (*'s* in English)
El libro **DEL** niño (but: **de la** niña, **de los** niños, **de las** niñas)

2. UN and EL instead of UNA and LA:

In front of feminine singular nouns with initial **a-, á-** or **ha-** stressed.

UN or EL as special feminine singular forms	**Normal** in the **plural** and/or when *preceded by an adjective:*
EL agua (water) **UN** arma (weapon) **EL** hambre (hunger)	las agu*as*; la *fresca* agua un*as* arm*as*; una *vieja* arma una *terrible* hambre

Note: ningún and **algún** are used instead of **ninguna** and **alguna** in the same circumstances.

3. Neuter LO: do not confuse with object pronoun *LO*, §12.

(a) **LO** + **masculine adjective:** expresses the essence of an adjective as a noun phrase.
Lo bueno es que estamos sanos y salvos
= *The good thing* is that we are safe and sound.
Lo esencial es tener éxito = *The essential thing* is to succeed.

(b) **LO** + **superlative adverb** + **posible/que puede:** See §27.

C. THE INDEFINITE ARTICLE: USAGE

1. When used in Spanish but not in English:
With an abstract noun qualified by an adjective
Estudiaba con **UNA** concentración total
= He was studying with ___ total concentration.

2. When omitted in Spanish but used in English:

(a) Job, nationality, religion

Es ___ dentista.   Es ___ francés.   Eres ___ cristano.
He is **A** dentist.   He is **A** Frenchman. You are **A** Christian.

(b) In apposition.
Barcelona, __ ciudad internacional, tiene un gran aeropuerto.
Barcelona, **AN** international city, has a big airport.

(c) ___ **Otro** = **AN**other; __ Cien = **A** hundred; __ Mil = **A** thousand;
Tal __ hombre = such **A** man; ¡Qué __ escuela! = What **A** school!

3. Unos, unas = some/any: See §20.

D. THE DEFINITE ARTICLE: USAGE

1. When used in Spanish but not in English:

(a) Before nouns used non-specifically:
La carne es muy cara = __ Meat is very expensive.
Busco **la** seguridad   = I am looking for __ security.

(b) Titles, ranks; (el) señor and names
El Rey Enrique __ Segundo   *Note:* The article is omitted
= __ King Henry the Second   before the number.
El capitán Álvarez = __ Captain Álvarez
  Note also: ¡**La** pobre María! = Poor Mary!

| Mr | : | **El señor José *PÉREZ* Salvador**★ | ★Formal title includes the mother's surname |

Mr :	**El señor José *PÉREZ* Salvador**★
+	
Miss :	La señorita María *RUIZ* Rodríguez★
↓	
Mrs :	La señora *PÉREZ* (least formal); La senora DE PÉREZ; La señora María *RUIZ DE PÉREZ* (very formal)
Mr and Mrs :	Los señores *PÉREZ* or El señor *PÉREZ* y su mujer/señora

★Formal title includes the mother's surname

Note 1: The article is omitted in direct address:
       ¡Adiós, __ señor Pérez . . . __ capitán Álvarez!

Note 2: *don/doña* before a Christian name shows respect:
       Buenos días, *don* Fernando

(c) Parts of the body and clothing — instead of the possessive adjective.
Cerró **los** ojos = He closed his eyes.
Se ponen **el** abrigo = They put on their overcoats.
                    (Singular, because they each have one).

Note 1: Action to one's own person: reflexive pronoun
Me lavo las manos = I wash my hands (myself).

Note 2: Action to another person: indirect object pronoun.
Le lavo las manos (**a él, a ella, a usted**).
= I wash his/her/your hands. (See §13, a + disjunctive)

(d) With countries and languages: See §29.

§26 COLOURS

white	=	blanco
black	=	negro
red	=	rojo
green	=	verde
blue	=	azul
grey	=	gris
yellow	=	amarillo
mauve	=	morado
purple	=	purpúreo
brown	=	marrón

hair: blond = rubio; brown = castaño.

pink	=	(color) *rosa*★
orange	=	(color) *naranja*★; anaranjado
light blue	=	*azul claro*★;
dark blue	=	*azul oscuro*★

★No agreement
ojos *azul oscuro*
pañuelos (color) *naranja*; anaranjados
camisas (color) *rosa*;

---

§27 COMPARATIVE AND SUPERLATIVE

A. COMPARATIVE

1. Adjectives: *more* difficult/tall*er*(than); *less* tall (than); *as* tall *as*.

Pedro es **más** alto **que** Juan = taller than John.
María es **menos** alta (f.) **que** Luisa = less tall than Louise.
Son **tan** altos (pl.) **como** ellos = as tall as them.

2. Adverbs: *more* slowly (than); *less* skilfully (than); *as* well *as*

Trabajo **más** lentamente **que** él = more slowly than him.
Trabaja **menos** hábilmente **que** Juan = less skilfully than John.
Escribe **tan** bien **como** Ana = as well as Anne.

Note 1: Tanto, -a, -os, -as + nouns:
Tengo tantas flores como Anita = I have as many flowers as Anita.

Note 2: más/menos DE + numbers e.g.: más DE veinte

B. SUPERLATIVE

1. Adjectives: *the most* pretty/prett*iest*; *the least* useful

— add **el, la, los, las** to the comparative **más**:
Esa chica es **la** más guapa = the most pretty/prettiest.
Esos son **los** menos útiles = the least useful
Los peores * crímenes   = the worst crimes (*See D below)
        └────── note accent gain — see §43

Note 1: Superlative after the noun — omit the article:
      La historia ____ más aburrida = The most (*or* more) boring
      story.

Note 2: El edificio más grande **DEL** país. (*De* = in after a
      superlative).

2. Adverbs: the most ____ ly; the least ____ ly

Trabajo **más** rápidamente = I work the most (*or* more) quickly.
Trabaja **menos** hábilmente = He works the least (*or* less) skilfully.

Note: The superlative adverb is identical to the comparative form.
LO may be used in conjunction with *posible* or *que + poder*:
Conduzco **LO** más cuidadosamente *posible/que puedo*.
= I drive as carefully as possible/as I can.

C. THE ABSOLUTE SUPERLATIVE: most, extremely

1. Adjectives: add -ísimo (or simply use muy + adjective)

caro → carísimo; rico → riquísimo (note spelling change)

2. Adverbs: add -ísimamente (or muy + adverb)

clarísimamente   but: very much is *muchísimo*

D. IRREGULAR COMPARATIVES AND SUPERLATIVES

1. Simple adjective	Comparative	Superlative

bueno   = good
malo   = bad
grande   = big
pequeño = small
	mejor = better
	peor = worse
	mayor = older; greater*
	menor = younger;
	           smaller, less*
		el mejor = the best
		el peor = the worst
		el mayor = (the oldest
		          (the greatest
		el menor = (the youngest
		          (the least

*Note 1: Greater/est, less/least in degree, e.g. de mayor importancia = of
       greater importance.
Note 2: (el) **más grande** and (el) **más pequeño** relate to size.
Note 3: See §22 for the agreement of mej**OR**, etc.

2. Simple Adverb		Comparative		Superlative	
bien	= well	mejor	= better	(lo) mejor	= the best
mal	= badly	peor	= worse	(lo) peor	= the worst
mucho	= a lot/much	más	= more	(lo) más	= the most
poco	= a little	menos	= less	(lo) menos	= the least

Note: Adverbs are invariable.

§28 CONJUNCTIONS

1. Y = and. Y changes to **E** before *i* and *hi* (but not *hie*)

e.g.: españoles **E** ingleses; mentiras **E hi**storias
But: acero Y **hie**rro

2. O = or. O changes to **U** before *o* or *ho*

e.g. fábricas U **o**ficinas; muchachos U **ho**mbres

3. Sino = but: after a *negative*, **sino** introduces a *contradiction*

No es valiente **sino** cobarde = He is *not* brave, but cowardly

Note: *sino que* + *verb*:
No habla **sino que** grita = He doesn't talk, but shouts.

Otherwise, pero is used to introduce additional information (with **sí** added for emphasis):
No es valiente **pero (sí)** es decidido .... but (he is) determined.

§29 COUNTRIES, LANGUAGES, INHABITANTS

Los países = the countries

> **el idioma; el/la habitante,
> el adjetivo: agreement, §22.**

Europa	=	Europe	europeo
España	=	Spain	español
(la) Gran Bretaña	=	Great Britain	británico
(el) Reino Unido	=	U.K.	
Inglaterra	=	England	inglés
Escocia	=	Scotland	escocés
(el País de) Gales	=	Wales	galés
Irlanda	=	Ireland	irlandés
Francia	=	France	francés
Bélgica	=	Belgium	belga
Alemania	=	Germany	alemán
Holanda	=	Holland	holandés
Italia	=	Italy	italiano

Portugal	= Portugal	portugués
Austria	= Austria	austriaco
Suiza	= Switzerland	suizo
Rusia (la) Unión Soviética }	= Russia	ruso
(los) Estados Unidos	= U.S.A.	{ estadounidense norteamericano
(el) Canadá	= Canada	canadiense
(la) América del Sur Sudamérica }	= South America	sudamericano
(la) (República) Argentina	= Argentina	argentino
Méjico	= Mexico	mejicano
(el) Perú	= Peru	peruano
(el) Brasil	= Brazil	brasileño
África	= Africa	africano
Australia	= Australia	australiano
Nueva Zelanda	= New Zealand	novozelandés
(el) Japón	= Japan	japonés

Note 1: Capital letters for countries only. (See also §21.B)

Note 2: The article is used with some countries, as indicated above in brackets: en **el** Japón; **del** Canadá; **al** Perú.

Note 3: The article is normally used with languages:
Conocer **el** español es útil. Aprendo **el** francés.
But: The article is omitted after **hablar** ... unless qualified.
Habla ____ español ... habla **bien el** español.

§30 *DAR* IDIOMS

dar a = to overlook   e.g. La ventana daba a la calle.
dar gritos = to shout   Están dando gritos.
dar la hora = to strike the hour   Dan las dos.
dar con = to run into/meet by chance   Dio con su amigo.
dar un paseo (... en coche) = to go for a walk (... a drive)
dar los buenos días a = to say good morning/hello to somebody
dar las gracias a = to thank somebody
    e.g. Tengo que dar las gracias a mi tío por el regalo.
darse cuenta de = to realise
    e.g. Me di cuenta de* que había salido. (*§40. Note 1)
        = I realised that he had gone out.

§31 DATE, DAYS, MONTHS, YEAR, SEASONS

A. Date (*la fecha*)

el primero de marzo ... use the *ordinal number* for the 1st.
or el (día) uno de marzo
el dos → el treinta y uno ... use *cardinal numbers*.

B. Days of the Week
(los días de la semana)

lunes	viernes
martes	sábado
miércoles	domingo
jueves	

C. Months of the Year
(los meses del año)

enero	julio
febrero	agosto
marzo	septiembre
abril	octubre
mayo	noviembre
junio	diciembre

Note 1: the small initial letters.

Note 2: en febrero *or* en el mes de febrero = In February.

Note 3: See also *expressions of time*, §64.4

D. Year *(el año)*

En mil novecientos ochenta y cuatro = in 1984.

El veinticinco **de** junio **de** mil novecientos cincuenta y tres.

↓

On 25th June, 1953

El Año Nuevo = The New Year
El día de Año Nuevo = New Year's Day

E. Seasons of the Year *(las estaciones del año)*

en (la) primavera	= in (the) spring	en (el) otoño	= in (the) autumn
en (el) verano	= in (the) summer	en (el) invierno	= in (the) winter

§32 DEBER, TENER QUE, HABER DE, HAY QUE

1. DEBER: *must, should, ought to*; *have/had* to★
    deber suggests *morally obliged to . . . supposed to*

Present: **Debo** trabajar = I *must* (ought to, have to) work.

Future: **Deberé** comenzar mañana = I *must* (shall have to) start tomorrow.

Preterite: (event)
Debió terminarlo antes de acostarse.
= He *had to* finish it before going to bed.

Imperfect: (state)
El alumno sabía que **debía** estudiar mucho.
= The pupil knew that he *should* (was supposed to) [had to] study hard.
Cuando llovía, **debíamos** jugar en el garaje (. . . pero continuábamos jugando en el jardín).
= When it rained, we *were supposed* to [had to] play in the garage, (. . . but we carried on playing in the garden).

Perfect:
He debido hacer la compra hoy, porque mi mujer está enferma.
= I *have had* to do the shopping today, because my wife is ill.
★Note: when have/had to means compelled to, use tener que

Pluperfect:
Habíamos debido castigarle porque había mentido.
= We *had had* to punish him because he had lied.

Conditional: ought to, *should*
Debería (**or** *debiera*) ayudarles = I ought to/should help them.

Conditional Perfect: ought to have, should have
Habría (**or** *hubiera*) **debido** traerlos
Debería (**or** *debiera*) **haberlos** traído $\Big\}$ = I ought to have brought them

Note 1: the *-ra form of the Imperfect Subjunctive* may be used instead of the conditional tenses. (§62)

Note 2: **Deber** also means *to owe*: Nos debe mucho dinero.

Note 3: **Deber DE** states a *supposition*:
Debe **DE** llegar en el tren de las cinco.
= He *must be* (is probably) coming on the 5 o'clock train.
¡Están borrachos! — $\Big\{$Debieron **DE** Han debido **DE** $\Big\}$ beberse todo el vino.
= They're drunk! — They *must have* drunk all the wine.

2. TENER QUE + **infinitive:** have to/must — i.e. compelled.

Tiene que terminarlo = He *has to/must* finish it.
Tuve que reparar el motor = I *had to* repair the engine.

3. HABER DE + **infinitive:** to be (supposed) to — weaker than deber.

He de llevar una corbata = I *am supposed* to wear a tie.
Habéis de terminar antes de salir = You *are* (*supposed*) to finish before leaving.

4. HAY QUE + **infinitive:** it is necessary to; one must ...

(Also: **es preciso** + infinitive; **es preciso que** + subjunctive, §62)

Hay que estudiar para aprobar.
= It is necessary to study in order to pass.

Había que soportar las condiciones.
= It was necessary to (we, you etc. had to) endure the conditions.

§33 DIMENSIONS AND DISTANCE

1. Dimensions: tener + dimension + de + adjective or noun

DE +	length	width	height	depth	thickness
adjective	largo	ancho	alto	★	★
or noun	longitud	anchura	altura	profundidad	espesor

La torre Eiffel tiene 320 metros **de alto** (**de altura**).
La cocina tiene cuatro metros **de largo** (**de longitud**).
La muralla tiene un metro *de espesor.**
El río tiene diez metros *de profundidad.**   }   *The noun is more normal.*

2. Distance

¿Qué distancia hay de nuestra casa **a** la biblioteca?. . .(**a** = **to**)
= How far is it from our house to the library?
La biblioteca está **a** tres kilometros. . .(**a** suggests away)

§34 DIMINUTIVES AND AUGMENTATIVES

1. Examples of diminutives

(a) -ito, -cito, -ecito:
express smallness and/or affection:

pequeñito = very tiny
la mujercita = (dear) little
woman
el viejecito = little old man

(b) -illo, -cillo, -ecillo:
express small size:

el cigarillo = cigarette
el rinconcillo = small corner
el panecillo = (bread) roll

(c) -uelo, -zuelo, -ezuelo: *express smallness and often contempt:*
el autorzuelo = small-time writer, "scribbler"

2. Examples of augmentatives

(a) -ón/-ona: *expresses largeness:* el muchachón = oversized boy

(b) -azo/-aza: *expresses hugeness:* un gatazo = a large cat

(c) -ote/a, acho/a: *suggest largeness and sometimes contempt:*
palabrotas = vulgar expressions   la mujeracha = a large coarse woman

§35 GUSTAR, AND SIMILAR VERBS

Gustar, to please, usually translates *to like* (things), as indicated in the literal English translations below:

English Subject	Verb	Direct Object	Indirect Object	Verb	Spanish Subject
I	like	painting	**Me** To me	*gusta* is pleasing	pintar painting
Mary	likes	the flowers	**A María le*** To Mary	*gustan* are pleasing	las flores the flowers

*Note 1: The indirect object is repeated in pronoun form. (§12.6)

 Note 2: Querer is to like/love people: Quiere a su novio.

Similar constructions with: **quedar, hacer falta, faltar, sobrar.**

We have two pounds left $\left\{\begin{array}{l}\text{Nos } \textit{quedan} \text{ dos libras.} \\ \text{Two pounds remain to us.}\end{array}\right.$

He needs a watch .... $\left\{\begin{array}{l}\text{Le } \text{hace falta un reloj.} \\ \text{A watch is necessary to him.}\end{array}\right.$

I am short of petrol ...... $\left\{\begin{array}{l}\text{Me } \textit{falta} \text{ gasolina.} \\ \text{Petrol is lacking to me.}\end{array}\right.$
| **or,** *more simply:* |
| Necesito gasolina. |

They have more than ..... $\left\{\begin{array}{l}\text{Les } \textit{sobra} \text{ comida.} \\ \text{Food is enough for their needs.}\end{array}\right.$
enough food

Note also: *doler* = to hurt/to have an ache in:

I have earache .... $\left\{\begin{array}{l}\text{Me } \textit{duele} \text{ el oído.} \\ \text{My ear hurts me.}\end{array}\right.$

§36 HABER

A. HABER IN THE 3rd PERSON SINGULAR

1. There is/are

hay	= there is/are	habrá	= there will be
había	= there was/were (state)	habría	= there would be
hubo	= there was/were (action)	ha habido	= there has/have been.

Hay una regla sobre la mesa.
= There is a ruler on the table (statement of fact).

Note 1: *There's ...! There are ...!* (demonstrating)
¡Allí está tu regla! = There's your ruler!

Note 2: *Here's ...! Here are ...!*
¡Aquí están los libros! = Here are the books!

2. **Hay que** + infinitive: One, he, you, we (etc.) must ... (§32)

3. **Hay:** used in some weather expressions (§65)

B. HABER FULLY CONJUGATED

1. Used to form the Compound Tenses (§6 – 10) and the *Perfect Infinitive* (§47)

2. **Haber de** + infinitive: *am* (*supposed*) *to* (§32)

§37 HAVE/HAD JUST: FOR AND CONTINUING TIME

Basic Pattern:

ENGLISH	SPANISH
Perfect Tense ⟶	Present Tense
Pluperfect Tense ⟶	Imperfect Tense

1. HAVE/HAD just: acabar de + infinitive
(a) I **HAVE JUST** bought it = **Acabo de** comprarlo ... *Spanish Present*
(b) They **HAD JUST** sold it = **Acababan de** venderlo ... *Spanish (Imp.)*

2. FOR ... and continuing time

(a) *Perfect → Present* $\Big\{$ **HACE** (*time*) **QUE** (*verb*)
                                      (*verb*) **DESDE HACE** (*time*)
How long HAVE you BEEN here?
¿Cuánto tiempo hace que (or, ¿Desde cuándo...) estás aquí?
HACE *tres días* **QUE** *estoy* aquí. $\Big\}$ = I **HAVE BEEN** here
Estoy aquí **DESDE HACE** *tres días.* $\quad$ for three days.

(b) *Pluperfect → Imperfect* $\Big\{$ **HACÍA** (*time*) **QUE** (*verb*)
                                            (*verb*) **DESDE HACÍA** (*time*)
How long HAD you BEEN playing there?
¿Cuánto tiempo hacía que (or, ¿Desde cuándo...) jugabas allí?
HACÍA *diez minutos* **QUE** *jugaba* allí. $\Big\}$ = I **HAD BEEN** playing
Jugaba allí **DESDE HACÍA** *diez minutos.* $\quad$ there for ten minutes.

Note 1: The verb may be in the Continuous Tense.
e.g. jugaba → estaba jugando

Note 2: **Llevar** + *present participle* may also be used:
Llevan (llevaban) un cuarto de hora nadando.
They HAVE (HAD) BEEN swimming for a quarter of an hour.

Note 3: **Since**...: *Present/Imperfect* + *desde* + time.
Espero (or llevo esperando) desde las dos.
= I HAVE BEEN waiting SINCE 2 o'clock.
Esperaba (or llevaba esperando) desde las dos.
= I HAD BEEN waiting SINCE 2 o'clock.

Note 4: *completed duration:* for = *por* or *durante* (§45)

Note 5: **hace** = *ago:* **Hace** muchos años = Many years *ago.*

§38 IMPERATIVE AND POLITE COMMANDS

1. Tú form imperative (affirmative)

Use the 3rd person singular of the present tense:

-ar	: ¡Habla!	= Speak!
-er	: ¡Vende!	= Sell!
-ir	: ¡Vive!	= Live!
R.C.V.:	¡Piensa!	= Think!
R.C.V.:	¡Pide!	= Ask for ...!
R.C.V.:	¡Duerme!	= Sleep!

NEGATIVE: No + *tú* form of PRESENT SUBJUNCTIVE (§62)

¡No hablES!	= Don't speak!
¡No vendAS!	= Don't sell!
¡No vivAS!	= Don't live!
¡No piensES!	= Don't think!
¡No pidAS!	= Don't ask!
¡No duermAS!	= Don't sleep!

Exceptions

		NEGATIVE — SUBJUNCTIVE			NEGATIVE — SUBJUNCTIVE
decir	: DI	No digas	salir	: SAL	No salgas
hacer	: HAZ	No hagas	ser	: SÉ	No seas
ir	: VE	No vayas	tener	: TEN	No tengas
poner	: PON	No pongas	venir	: VEN	No vengas
reír	: RÍE	No rías			

Other irregular verbs follow the normal rule:

huir	: huye	No huyas	estar	: está	No estés
oír	: oye	No oigas	ver	: ve★	No veas

(★identical form to: ve = go)

2. Vosotros form imperative

Change the infinitive R → D: no exceptions.
Negative: No + *vosotros* form of present subjunctive.

¡Hablad!	= Speak!	No habléis	¡Estad!	= Be!	No estéis
¡Vended!	= Sell!	No vendáis	¡Sed!	= Be!	No seáis
¡Vivid!	= Live!	No viváis	¡Decid!	= Tell!	No digáis

¡Estad allí a las dos! = Be there at 2 o'clock!
¡Sed buenos! = Be good!

3. Polite commands: Usted(es) forms:

— *Use the 3rd person forms of the present subjunctive.*

-ar : HablE Vd.	**-er :** VendA Vd.	**-ir :** VivA Vd.
HablEN Vds.	VendAN Vds.	VivAN Vds.

Irregular verbs, e.g. *hacer* : HagA Vd.   poner : PongA Vd.
(same rule)   HagAN Vds.   PongAN Vds.

Negative: *simply place* **no** *before the affirmative:*
¡No hable usted! = Don't speak!   ¡No pongan...! = Don't put...!

Note: The pronouns *Vd.* and *Vds.* are not always used, but it is more polite to do so.

4. Let us (Let's)

(a) Use the *nosotros* form of the present subjunctive.
¡TrabajEMOS juntos! = Let's work together!
Negative: ¡No trabajEMOS juntos! = Don't let's work together!

or **(b) Vamos a** + *infinitive* (affirmative only):
¡Vamos a trabajar juntos! = Let's work together!

5. Let him..., May he...: Que + 3rd person present subjunctive — suggests permission, and may also imply a wish or hope:

Que lea Pedro = Let Peter read.
¡Que termine María! = May Mary finish!

Note: *let = allow:* **dejar** or **permitir.**
        ¡Déjeme Vd. terminarlo! = Let me finish it! (permission)

6. Position of object pronouns

	Affirmative: *attached*		**Negative:** *precede*
tú	¡Háblanos!	= Speak to us!	¡No nos hables!
vosotros	¡Vendedlos!	= Sell them!	¡No los vendáis!
usted(es)	¡Muéstre(n)selo!	= Show it him!	¡No se lo muestre(n)!
nosotros	¡Traigámoslos!	= Let's bring them!	¡No los traigamos!

7. Reflexive imperatives

	Affirmative: *attached*		**Negative:** *precede*
tú	¡Lávate!	= Wash!	¡No te laves!
vosotros	¡Láva __ os!	= Wash!	¡No os lavéis!
usted(es)	¡Láve(n)se!	= Wash!	¡No se lave(n)!
nosotros	¡Lavémo __ nos!	= Let us wash!	¡No nos lavemos!

Note 1: **d** is removed before **os**, e.g. ¡Senta __ os! = Sit down! (*Exception:* ¡Idos! = Go away!)
        -ir verbs take an accent before **os** ¡Vestí __ os! = Get dressed!

Note 2: **s** is removed before **nos**
        e.g. ¡Vámo __ nos! = Let's go away! ¡Sentémo __ nos! = Let's sit down!

§39 IMPERSONAL VERBS

1. They exist in the third person singular only, e.g.

Weather verbs: llueve (está lloviendo) etc. (§65) hay (que), §36.

2. Many verbs may be used impersonally, e.g.

Más vale que = It is better that ...
Es posible que = It is possible that ...
No importa = It doesn't matter.

§40 INFINITIVES

A. VERBS — HOW LINKED TO INFINITIVES

1. Direct link

(a) Common examples

deber	= to have to	parecer	= to seem to
decidir	= to decide to	pensar	= to intend to
desear	= to wish/desire to	poder	= to be able to
esperar	= to hope/expect to	preferir	= to prefer to
evitar	= to avoid doing	prometer	= to promise to
lograr	= to manage to	querer	= to want to
necesitar	= to need to	saber	= to know (how to)
negar	= to refuse to	soler	= to be accustomed to;
olvidar	= to forget to		"usually" (§24)
		temer	= to fear to.

Espero ganar. Debo cambiar este billete.

(b) After: mandar, ordenar, hacer; dejar, permitir; aconsejar; impedir, prohibir. These may take a *direct infinitive* or a *subjunctive construction* (§62B.1 & 10)

Te aconsejo probarlo
Aconsejo que lo pruebes $\Big\}$ = I advise you to try it.

Note 1: *Hacer + infinitive:* to make someone do something
Le hice esperar = I make him wait.
Note 2: *Mandar + infinitive:* to have something done
Mandé construir un garaje = I had a garage built.
Note 3: *Dejar caer* = to drop (let fall): Dejé caer el libro.

(c) After verbs of seeing and hearing (perception)
La vimos nadar (*or* nadando, §41) = We saw her swimming.
To hear (tell) that: He oído decir que es perezoso.
To hear (speak) of: He oído hablar de ella.

(d) After impersonal constructions: Es fácil hacerlo.

2. Linked by A

(a) Common examples

animar a	= to encourage to	forzar a★	= to force to
acostumbrarse a	= to get accustomed to	invitar a	= to invite to
aprender a	= to learn to	ir a	= to be going to
atreverse a	= to dare to		(§2)
ayudar a	= to help to	negarse a	= to refuse to
comenzar a	= to begin to	obligar a★	= to oblige to
decidirse a	= to decide to	pararse a	= to stop to
disponerse a	= to get ready to	persuadir a★	= to persuade to
empezar a	= to begin to	ponerse a	= to begin to

enseñar a	= to teach to	prepararse a	= to prepare to
		volver a	= to return to, "again" (§24)

Comenzaremos **a** estudiar mañana.

(*or forzar a que, obligar a que, persuadir a que + subjunctive).

(b) Verbs of motion
ir: to go (and); **venir:** to come (and); **correr**, etc.
Voy **a** visitarle cada día. Corrí **a** verla.

3. Linked by DE

acabar de	= to have just (§37)	excusar(se) de	= to excuse from -ing
acordarse de	= to remember to	guardarse de	= to take care not to
alegrarse de	= to be pleased to	haber de	= to have to (§32)
cansarse de	= to get tired -ing	olvidarSE de	= to forget to
cesar de	= to cease -ing	parar de	= to stop -ing
dejar de	= to stop -ing	terminar de	= to finish -ing
no dejar de	= not to fail to	tratar de	= to try to

Cesaron **de** charlar = They stopped chatting.

4. Linked by EN, CON, POR:

consentir en	= to consent to	interesarse en	= to be interested in doing
convenir en	= to agree to		
divertirse en	= to amuse oneself -ing	ocuparse en	= to be busy -ing
		pensar en	= to think of -ing
esforzarse en (or por)	= to strive to	tardar en	= to be long -ing
		vacilar en	= to hesitate to
insistir en	= to insist on	soñar con	= to dream of -ing
amenazar con	= to threaten		

Verbs of beginning and finishing + **POR = BY. . .-ING**
Empecé/terminé POR gritar = I began/finished by shouting.

5. Para = in order to: implies purpose

Se detuvo para comprar huevos = He stopped (in order) to buy eggs.
Note also: demasiado cansado PARA correr = too tired to run.
              bastante pequeño PARA caber = small enough to fit.

B. NOUNS AND ADJECTIVES LINKED TO INFINITIVES

1. De is the most common:

Siento vergüenza **de** admitirlo. Estoy contento **de** hacerlo.

2. A, EN, POR are occasionally used

obligado **A** hacerlo; el primero/último **EN** salir; tener prisa **POR** comerlo.

Note 1: Linking prepositions are retained before a **que** clause:
Estoy encantado **de que** hayas venido.
Me olvidé **de que** había llegado.

Note 2: nada/algo/mucho **QUE** hacer
= nothing/something/a lot to do.

§41 -ING: HOW TO TRANSLATE

1. By the Present Participle

(a) Estar + present participle
Estoy hablando = I am talking.
(**Also:** continuar, seguir, ir and venir + present participle — see §52, the
progressive tenses)

(b) Standing alone:
— *Relating to the subject*
Él trabajaba, **soñando** con sus vacaciones.
= He worked, dreaming of his holidays.

Siendo ministro, tenía muchas responsabilidades.
= Being a minister, he had many responsibilities.

Comiendo menos, adelgazarás.
= By eating less, you will lose weight.

— *Relating to the direct object*, after a verb of perception

Vi a Pedro **nadando** en el mar. | **or** *nadar*, 2(e) below;
= I saw Peter swimming in the sea. | **or** *que nadaba*, 3 below.

Note 1: salir/bajar/subir + corriendo = to run out/down/up:
Salió corriendo del cine   = He ran out of the cinema.
Bajó la escalera corriendo = He ran down the stairs.

Note 2: Habiendo + past participle:
Habiendo estudiado todo el año . . . = Having studied all year. . . (See also §47)

2. By the Infinitive

(a) al + infinitive = on . . . -ing.
Al terminar el trabajo salió = On finishing the work he went out.

(b) after main verbs (see §40)
Evita hacer sus deberes = He avoids doing his homework.
Se puso a escribirlo = He set about writing it.

(c) Preposition + infinitive:
Examples
sin   = without : sin comprenderlo = without understanding it.
antes de   = before : antes de llegar   = before arriving.
después de = after   : después de verla = after seeing her.

(d) The infinitive used as a noun.
Le gusta **cantar** = He likes singing.
El ladrar del perro = The barking of the dog.

(e) The infinitive is also used after verbs of perception. (See §40.1.c)
Vi nadar al chico = I saw the boy swimming.
La escuchaba (la veía) leer = I listened to her (saw her) reading.

3. Que + clause

Tengo una teoría **que explica** el problema (*not* explicando)
= I have a theory explaining (= which explains) the problem.

Vi al chico **que nadaba** en la piscina.
= I saw the boy who was swimming in the pool.

4. By a past participle, when defining state or position (Agreement + subject)

sentado   = sitting (see §59)   apoyado   = leaning
dormido   = sleeping   colgado   = hanging
acostado   = lying (in bed)   arrodillado = kneeling
incorporado = sitting up (in bed)   inclinado   = bending down.

La dejé **arrodillad*a*** en la iglesia = I left her kneeling in the church.

5. By many adjectives

e.g: **interesante** = interesting   **atractivo** = inviting

Note: Two (invariable) present participles may be used adjectively:
ardiendo = burning: (la) cara ardiendo = very hot face
hirviendo = boiling: el aceite hirviendo = the boiling oil

§42 NEGATIVES

1. Simple negation: place **no** before the **verb** (*or object pronoun*)
No puedo hacerlo = I cannot do it.
No *los* hemos vendido = We have not sold them.

2. Negatives which may precede or follow the verb

nunca (or jamás) = never   ninguno (adjective) = no + noun
nada   = nothing   (pronoun) = not any/none
nadie   = nobody   ni ... ni = neither ... nor
tampoco   = neither   ni, ni siquiera = not even.

Before the verb	No + verb + negative
Nunca los como.	No los vendí jamás.
= I never eat them.	= I never sold them.
Nada ocurre.	No he visto nada.
= Nothing happens.	= I have seen nothing.
Nadie ha hablado.	No oí **a** nadie. (Personal a, §48)
= Nobody has spoken.	= I heard nobody.
Ninguno sobrevivió.	No quiero ningún problema.
= None (not one) survived.	= I don't want any trouble.
Ni pedro **ni** María llegaron.	No tengo ni lápiz ni regla.
= Neither Peter nor Mary arrived.	= I have neither pencil nor ruler.

Note: As objects, **nada, nadie** and **ninguno** rarely precede the verb except for emphasis: e.g. **Nada** deseo = I want *nothing*.

3. Combination of negatives ... in English only one negative word:

No gastábamos **nunca nada** = We *never* wasted anything.
No vi a **nadie** en **ninguna** parte = I did*n't* see anybody anywhere.
¡**Ni** yo **tampoco**! = *Nor* me either!

4. Negatives standing alone

¿Quién lo vio? — **Nadie.**   Who saw it? — Nobody
¿Qué dijiste? — **Nada.**   What did you say? — Nothing.

5. Other negatives

ya no = no longer.   **no** ... **más que** = only
Ya no trabaja = He no longer works.
No tengo *más que* veinte discos = I have only 20 records
or Sólo tengo veinte discos   (... a *definite number*)

But: No tengo *más* **de** veinte discos = (I have no more than 20 records
                    (... in fact probably *fewer than* 20)

6. ¿(no es) verdad? = aren't we? Weren't you? etc.

Estamos ganando, ¿verdad?   = We're winning, aren't we?
Usted mentía, ¿no es verdad? = You were lying, weren't you?

7. not ... any/not a single/not any at all

No escribí cartas   = I didn't write (any) letters.
No escribí ninguna carta   = I didn't write *any* letters.
No escribí ni una sola carta = I didn't write *a single* letter.
No escribí carta **alguna**   = I didn't write *any* letters *at all*.
       ↖— functions negatively *after* the noun.

8. Negative imperative — see §38

§43 NOUNS

A. PLURAL OF NOUNS

1. Ending in a VOWEL: add -S

la mesa → las mesaS; el hombre → los hombreS; el chico → los chicoS

Note: -S is added to accented -á, -é, and -ó:
mamáS; papáS; caféS; dominóS
but: **-ES** is added to accented -ú or -í: tisúES, iglúES; rubíES

2. Ending in a CONSONANT: add -ES

doctor: el doctor → los doctorES   quality: la calidad → las calidadES
king: el rey → los reyES   month: el mes → los mesES

Note 1: *unstressed final syllables ending in -S:* no change:
la/las crisis; el/los lunes, martes, miércoles, jueves, viernes

Note 2: *loss or gain of accent to preserve original sound:* (§21)
loss: la ambición → las ambiciones; el inglés → los ingleses
gain: el/la joven → los/las jóvenes

Note 3: *change of accented syllable in these two words:*
character: el carácter → los caracteres
diet: el régimen → los regímenes.

3. Ending in Z: changes to CES

voice: la voz → las voCES   pencil: el lápiz → los lápiCES

4. Compound Nouns

railway: el ferrocarril → los ferrocarrilES
corkscrew: el sacacorchos → los sacacorchos (**no change**)

5. Masculine plural forms — may include both genders:
los padres   = fathers; parents   ;   mother and father.
los hijos   = sons, children   ;   brother and sister.
los señores = gentlemen   ;   Mr and Mrs (§25)
los reyes   = kings; monarchs   ;   king and queen

Also: los primos (cousins), los nietos (grandchildren), etc.

Note: Family names are not made plural;
Los Fuent**e** = the Fuentes, the Fuente family.

B. GENDER OF NOUNS

(a) Some nouns ending in -a are masculine:
el día   = day   el idioma   = language
el mapa   = map   el poema   = poem
el pijama = pyjamas   el problema = problem
el planeta = planet   el programa = programme
el sofá   = sofa   el sistema = system
el tranvía = tram   el telegrama = telegramme

(b) Some nouns ending in -o are feminine:
la mano = hand; la radio = radio; la foto (*grafía*) = photo (*graph*)

(c) Certain nouns refer to males or females:

el/la turista	= tourist	la estrella	= film star	⎫ la for
el/la artista	= artist	la persona	= person	⎬ both sexes
el/la estudiante	= student	la víctima	= victim	⎭

(d) Changed gender, changed meaning:
el policía = policeman   la policía = police force
el guía   = guide   la guía   = guide book

§44 NUMBERS

A. CARDINAL NUMBERS

0	cero	20	**veinte**	60	**sesenta**
1	*uno*★	21	veinti*uno*★	61	sesenta y *uno*★
2	dos	22	veintidós	62	sesenta y dos
3	tres	23	veintitrés	70	**setenta**
4	cuatro	24	veinticuatro	71	setenta y *uno*★
5	cinco	25	veinticinco	72	setenta y dos
6	seis	26	veintiséis		
7	siete	27	veintisiete	80	**ochenta**
8	ocho	28	veintiocho	81	ochenta y *uno*★
9	nueve	29	veintinueve	82	ochenta y dos
10	**diez**	**30**	**treinta**	**90**	**noventa**
11	once	31	treinta y *uno*★	91	noventa y *uno*★
12	doce	32	treinta y dos	92	noventa y dos
13	trece	**40**	**cuarenta**	**100**	**ciento**★
14	catorce	41	cuarenta y *uno*★	101	ciento *uno*★
15	quince	42	cuarenta y dos	102	ciento dos
16	dieciséis	**50**	**cincuenta**		
17	diecisiete	51	cincuenta y *uno*★		
18	dieciocho	52	cincuenta y dos		
19	diecinueve				

Note these alternative forms:
16 – 19: diez y seis/siete/ocho/nueve
21 – 29: veinte y uno/dos/tres, etc.

200	doscientos, -as	1,000	mil
300	trescientos, -as	1,001	mil uno
400	cuatrocientos, -as	(*but*: Las mil y una noches = Arabian Nights)
500	**quinientos, -as**	1,200	mil doscientos
600	seiscientos, -as	2,000	dos mil ← not plural
700	**setecientos, -as**	(*but*: miles de/millares de = thousands of)
800	ochocientos, -as	1,000,000	un millón (de)
900	**novecientos, -as**	2,000,000	dos millones de

1. Apocopation (See also §22)

*uno → un: before masculine nouns
un perro; veintiún chicos; treinta y un minutos; ciento un coches.

ciento → cien: before any plural noun (or adjective + noun) and mil: cien árboles; cien grandes árboles; cien mil.

2. Agreement

uno → una: before feminine nouns
una hora, veintiuna pesetas, ciento una casas
200 → 900; os → as: novecientas fábricas

3. Use of y: between tens and units only

242: doscientos __ cuarenta y dos

4. English *a* not translated before *cien(to)* **and** *mil*

__ cien hombres = a hundred men; __ mil soldados = a thousand soldiers

B. ORDINAL NUMBERS

1st	primero	6th	sexto	20th	vigésimo
2nd	segundo	7th	séptimo	100th	centésimo
3rd	tercero	8th	octavo	1000th	milésimo
4th	cuarto	9th	noveno		
5th	quinto	10th	décimo		

1. Primero and **tercero** lose the **o** before a masculine singular noun (§22).

2. Ordinals agree with the noun and normally precede it.

3. Ordinals are rarely used beyond 10th, after which cardinals are used, usually after the noun:
La **quinta** hora = the fifth hour. La página **treinta y tres**.

C. EXPRESSIONS DE + NOUN

una decena de	= 10 or so	centenares de	} hundreds of
una docena de	= a dozen	cientos de	
una veintena de	= 20 or so		

§45 PARA AND POR

1. FOR ... PARA ... *or* ... POR?

PURPOSE (intent/direction) ⟵ 1. BASIC DISTINCTION ⟶ CAUSE

Ese bolígrafo es **PARA** mi amigo. = That pen is for my friend.	*out of, through:* Estudio **POR** gusto. = I study for pleasure.
Esta rueda es **PARA** tu coche. = This wheel is for your car.	*on behalf of:* Terminé el trabajo **POR** él. = I finished the work for him.
Estudio **PARA** aprobar. (PARA + infin.) = I study in order to pass.	

movement towards destination ⟵ 2. PLACES ⟶ *movement through/along/in*

Me pongo en camino **PARA** Barcelona. = I set off for Barcelona (or **hacia**, or **a**)	Andaba **POR** Las Ramblas. = I was walking through/along Las Ramblas

achieving an aim, future implied ⟵ 3. TIME ⟶ *duration of time**

Lo haré **PARA** el domingo. = I will do it for (= by) Sunday.	Estuvimos en Mallorca **POR** dos semanas. = We were in Mallorca for two weeks.

with what intention? ⟵ 4. WHY? ⟶ *through what cause?*

¿**PARA** qué examinas el motor? = Why are you examining the engine? — Porque quiero hallar la avería. = Because I want to find the fault. (i.e., PARA hallar la avería.)	¿**POR** qué examinas el motor? = Why are you examining the engine? — Porque no funciona. = Because it does not work.

*Note 1: *Durante* is sometimes used instead of *POR*
Trabajo por/durante dos horas cada mañana.
= I work for two hours every morning.

Note 2: Desde hace = for: See §37.

2. POR: more uses

By: in the *Passive* (§46): escrito por Cela = written by Cela.
By sea, road, air: Por mar, carretera, avión.
(*But:* normally **en** for means of transport: en avión/coche/tren.)

For price: por sesenta pesetas = for sixty pesetas.

Per: por ciento = per cent.

§46 PASSIVE VOICE

A. ACTION...AND RESULTING STATE

THE TRUE PASSIVE for ACTION: **SER** + PAST PARTICIPLE	STATE resulting from the ACTION: **ESTAR** + PAST PARTICIPLE
Present: Action/event El ladrón **es detenido** por un policía = The burglar is arrested by a policeman.	*Present: resulting state* El ladrón **está detenido**. = The burglar is arrested/under arrest.
Preterite: Action La oficina **fue abierta** por el jefe a las nueve. = The office was opened by the boss at 9 o'clock.	*Preterite: completed state* La oficina **estuvo abierta** por dos horas. = The office was open for two hours.
Imperfect: Habitual action La oficina **era abierta** cada mañana a las nueve. = The office was opened every morning at 9 o'clock. (Also: se abría...opened*)	*Imperfect: incompleted state* La oficina **estaba abierta** cuando él telefoneó. = The office was open when he telephoned. (and continued to remain open.)
Future: Action **Serán liberados** por las tropas. = They will be liberated by the troops.	*Future: State* **Estarán liberados** después de la victoria. = They will be free after the victory.
Conditional Perfect: Action La discoteca **habría sido abierta** por el conserje. = The disco would have been opened by the caretaker.	*Conditional Perfect: State* La discoteca **habría estado abierta**. = The disco would have been open.

Note 1: The past participle agrees with the subject.
Note 2: POR = by, referring to the agent
Note 3: A reflexive verb often replaces the passive, especially when the agent is not specified — see also B.2 below.

B. THE PASSIVE IS OFTEN AVOIDED IN SPANISH

1. Change the sentence: PASSIVE → *ACTIVE*

El anillo **fue examinado por el joyero** ... jeweller: **the agent**.
El joyero examinó el anillo (preferable) ... jeweller: *the subject*.

2. Use the reflexive form:

Aquí **se venden** peras = Pears are sold here.
Me llamo Pablo = I am called Pablo.
Se permiten perros = Dogs are allowed.

Note also: **Se dice** que... = It is said that...

3. Use a non-specific *they:*

Dicen que es loco = It is said (they say) that he is mad.
Comentan que se ha fugado = It is said that he has fled.

§47 PAST PARTICIPLE

1. Formation

Remove -AR: add -ADO habl**ADO** = spoken	Remove -ER or -IR: add -IDO vend**IDO** = sold viv**IDO** = lived

2. Irregular Past Participles

abrir	:	abierto	= opened	poner	:	puesto	= put
cubrir	:	cubierto	= covered	proveer	:	provisto	= provided
decir	:	dicho	= said	resolver	:	resuelto	= resolved
escribir	:	escrito	= written	romper	:	roto	= broken
freír	:	frito	= fried	ver	:	visto	= seen
hacer	:	hecho	= done/made	volver	:	vuelto	= returned
morir	:	muerto	= died				

Also compounds, e.g.: satisfecho = satisfied; supuesto = supposed

3. Uses

(a) **haber** + past participle: *Compound Tenses* (§6 – 10)

(b) To translate **-ING** in certain cases (§41)

(c) With **ser** or **estar** (*Passive* or *State*) (§46)

(d) **Perfect Infinitive:** (infinitive of haber + past participle)
Era importante **haberlo hecho** antes de la una.
= It was important to have finished it before one o'clock.

(e) **Having...ed**
Terminado el ejercicio, salió.
= Having finished the exercise, he went out.
(*or* **Habiendo terminado**...§41; *or* Cuando **había terminado**...§7)

§48 PERSONAL A

1. The Personal *a* is used before direct objects which are persons, whether nouns or pronouns.

Vio **a** tu padre ayer = He saw your father yesterday.
Encontré **a** María anoche = I met Mary last night.
Capturaron **al** ladrón (*a* + *el*) = They caught the thief.
Vi **al** que se escapó = I saw the one who escaped (Relative)
¿**A** quíen has visto? = Whom have you seen?   (Interrogative)
¡Detesta **a** ése! = He hates that man!   (Demonstrative)
No conozco **a** nadie = I know nobody.   (Indefinite)
Le vi **a** usted   = I saw you.   (Disjunctive)

Note: Personal *a* used before animals (pets):
    Acaraciaba **a** su perro = He stroked his dog.

2. When not used.

(a) **After** *tener* and *haber*:
Tiene ____ cinco primos.   Hay ____ dos hombres en mi oficina.

(b) **Before** *an unspecified person*: (Que clause + Subjunctive — see §62.B.7)
Busco ____ un fontanero = I am looking for a plumber.

§49 PODER, QUERER: SABER, CONOCER

1. Poder = To be able: can

Present   : Puede hacerlo = He can (= *is able to*) do it
Imperfect   : Podía hacerlo = He could (= *was able to*) do it
Conditional : Podría hacerlo = He could (= *would be able to/might*) do it

Note 1: ¿Puedo entrar? = *May* I come in? (requesting permission).

Note 2: Poder is often omitted with verbs of perception.
    Veo el árbol = I can see the tree.

Note 3: Poder is to be physically capable:
    Puedo nadar = I can swim (i.e. *no longer injured*)
    Saber is to have the "know-how":
    Sé nadar = I can swim (*because I have learned*)

2. Querer: *will* or *would* of requests (not the future *will*)

¿Quieres cambiarlo? = Will you (= *are you willing to*) change it?
(**or**, *more politely*: ¿Querría usted...? Would you...? — *Conditional*.
        ¿Quisiera usted...? Would you please...? — *Subjunctive*.)
No querían venir = They would not (= *they were unwilling to*) come.

3. Saber is to know facts:

Sé que tiene razón = I know that he is right.

4. Conocer is to know people and places:

Conozco bien $\left\{\begin{array}{l} \text{a María} \\ \text{Madrid} \end{array}\right.$ = I know Mary/Madrid well.

Note: conocer in the *preterite*: = to meet/make the acquaintance of
Conocí a Juan el año pasado = I (first) met John last year.

§50 PREPOSITIONS

1. A: to (*motion towards*)

Voy **A** casa, **A** la universidad, **A** España, **A** Santander.
= I go _____ home, to the university, to Spain, to Santander.

2. EN: at, in (*within*); on, into

Estoy **EN** casa, **EN** la universidad, **EN** España, **EN** Santander.
= I am at home, at (the) university, in Spain, in Santander.

Está **EN** el pupitre, **EN** la pared = It is on the desk, on the wall.
Entré **EN** la casa = I went into the house.

Note also:
EN avión, coche, bicicleta, etc. = By plane, car, bicycle, etc.
A pie = on foot; **A** caballo = On horseback.

3. DE: from

Soy **DE** Santander, **DE** España, **DEL** (§29) Canadá
Note: from one place to another: **DESDE** Burgos **HASTA** Oviedo.

4. Compound prepositions: certain adverbs + DE

antes de	= before (time)	dentro de	= inside
cerca de	= near	después de	= after
debajo de	= under (neath)	fuera de	= outside
delante de	= in front of	lejos de	= far from

Adverb: Está sentado **fuera** = He is sitting outside.
Preposition: Está esperando **fuera de** la tienda.
          = He is waiting outside the shop.

Adverb: Hice eso **antes** = I did that beforehand
Preposition: Lo hice **antes de salir** = I did it before going out

Note 1: the conjunction **antes (de) que** + subjunctive, §62.

Note 2: DE + adverb may provide adjectival function:
las ideas **DE antes** = previous (old) ideas
los problemas **DE ayer** = yesterday's problems.

§51 PREPOSITIONS: LINKING VERBS TO NOUNS OR PRONOUNS

1. "Built into" the Spanish

agradecer	= to be thankful **FOR**		mirar	= to look **AT**
buscar	= to look **FOR**		pedir	= to ask **FOR**
escuchar	= to listen **TO**		(See 2. below)	
esperar	= to wait **FOR**		señalar	= to point **TO**
			pagar	= to pay **FOR**

(Nos) agradecieron ____ la ayuda = They were grateful (to us) for the help.
Escuchaba ____ la radio = I was listening to the radio.
Pediré ____ un bolígrafo = I shall ask for a pen.
Pagó (un dólar POR) las flores = He paid (a dollar) for the flowers.
⌐——————— *use* **POR** if the amount is quoted.

2. A before the noun or pronoun

acercarse a	= to approach		saber a	= to taste of
asistir a	= to attend (watch)		subir a	= to get on (bus)
jugar a	= to play (sports)			
oler a	= to smell of		comprar a	= to buy ⌐
parecerse a	= to look like		robar a	= to steal | **something**
resistir a	= to resist		quitar a	= to take ⟩ **from a**
responder a	= to answer		tomar a	= to take ⌐ **person**

Juego **al** fútbol.
(*But*: Toco ____ la trompeta)
Subí **al** autobús.
= I got on the bus.

pedir a   = to ask [*to*] a person
                  FOR something
Le quitó el juguete **al** niño.
= He look the toy from the child.
Les pedí ____ un favor **a los** jefes
= I asked the bosses (for) a favour.

3. DE before the noun or pronoun

acordarse de	= to remember		despedirse de	= to say goodbye to
bajar de	= to get off (bus)		dudar de	= to doubt
burlarse de	= to make fun of		gozar de	= to enjoy
cambiar de	= to change (e.g. buses)		pensar de	= to think of (opinion)
carecer de	= to lack		quejarse de	= to complain about
compadecerse de	= to be sorry for		reírse de	= to laugh at
depender de	= to depend on		salir de	= to leave (e.g. house)
deshacerse de	= to get rid of		servirse de	= to make use of

Quiero deshacerme **de** esa basura = I want to get rid of that rubbish.
Cambié **de** autobuses = I changed buses.

But: Cambié ____ mis cheques de viajero/mi dinero.
¿Qué piensas de Anita? (opinion)

4. Others

beber en	= to drink from	casarse con	= marry
entrar en	= to enter	contar con	= to count on
fumar en	= to smoke a pipe	soñar con	= to dream of
pensar en	= to think (have in mind)		
reparar en	= to notice		

Pienso **en** Anita.   Puedes contar **con** Juan.

§52 PRESENT PARTICIPLE AND THE PROGRESSIVE TENSES

1. Formation of the Present Participle

Remove -AR: add -ANDO	:	hablANDO, speaking; dANDO, giving.
Remove -ER: add -IENDO	:	vendIENDO, selling; sIENDO, being.
Remove -IR: add -IENDO	:	vivIENDO, living; salIENDO, going out.

-IR Radical changing verbs

sIntiendo	=	feeling
mIntiendo	=	lying
dUrmiendo	=	sleeping
mUriendo	=	dying
pIdiendo	=	asking
rIendo	=	laughing
sIguiendo	=	following

Spelling change verbs

arguYendo	=	arguing
caYendo	=	falling
huYendo	=	fleeing
Yendo	=	going
leYendo	=	reading
oYendo	=	hearing
traYendo	=	bringing

Irregular verbs
dIciendo = saying; pUdiendo = being able; vIniendo = coming.

Note: The present participle is invariable.

2. The Progressive (continuous) Tenses: Estar + Present Participle

These forms emphasise the **ACTUALITY** or **DURATION** of the action.
Estoy trabajando ahora = I am working now ... **Actuality**
(**Contrast:** Trabajo cada mañana = I work every morning.)
Mientras *estábamos jugando* ... = While we were playing... **Duration**
(**Contrast:** Jugábamos cada día = We played every day.)

Note also: *continuar, seguir, ir and venir + present participle*:
Continúan estudiando = They are continuing to study/studying.
Siguieron buscando al culpable = They carried on looking for the culprit.
Va gritando por la playa = He is (going about) shouting on the beach.
Venían resbalándose en el hielo = They came slipping on the ice.

§53 PROBABILITY

Future: for present state	*Conditional:* for past state
Estará viajando solo. = I suppose he is (probably) travelling alone.	**Estaría nadando** solo cuando se ahogó. = He must have been (was probably) swimming alone when he drowned.
Future Perfect: recent action	*Conditional Perfect:* less recent action
Habrá destruido la prueba por ahora. = I suppose he has (probably) destroyed the evidence by now.	**Habría destruido** la prueba antes de que llegara la policía. = I suppose he had (probably) destroyed the evidence before the police came.

§54 PUNCTUATION

.	punto	" "	comillas
,	coma	—	raya (*dash*) used to introduce written dialogue
;	punto y coma		
:	dos puntos	-	guión (*hyphen*)
¡ !	signos de admiración	. . .	puntos suspensivos
¿ ?	signos de interrogación	( )	paréntesis

§55 RADICAL CHANGING VERBS: a summary

	1st, 2nd, 3rd sing. and 3rd plur. e → ie or o → ue			e → i	nosotros and vosotros stems:
	-AR	**-ER**	**-IR**	**PEDIR type**	
Present Indicative (§1)	pIEnso cUEnto	pIErdo vUElvo	sIEnto dUErmo	pIdo	as infinitive
Present Subjunctive (§62) *Also:* **Polite Commands** (§38)	pIEnse cUEnte	pIErda vUElva	sIEnta dUErma	pIda	-IR/pedir types: **SINT** -amos, -áis **DURM** -amos, -áis **PID** -amos, -áis
Imperative *Tú* **form** (§38)	pIEnsa cUEnta	pIErda vUElva	sIEnte dUErme	pIde	*vosotros* stem: as infinitive

	-IR/PEDIR types only		
	e → i		**o → u**
Preterite: *3rd* *persons only* (§5)	sIntió sIntieron	pIdió pIdieron	dUrmió dUrmieron
Imperfect Subjunctive (*throughout*) (§62)	{ sIntiera { sIntiese	pIdiera pIdiese	{ dUrmiera { dUrmiese
Present Participle (§52)	sIntiendo	pIdiendo	dUrmiendo

§56 REFLEXIVE VERBS

1. "Self" implied: the reflexive pronoun refers back to the subject.

levantar*se* :	**me** levanto	= I get [myself] up.
lavar*se* :	**te** lavas	= You wash [yourself]; get washed.
vestir*se* :	**se** viste	= He, she, you (pol.) get(s) dressed.
sentar*se* :	**nos** sentamos	= We sit [ourselves] down.
esconder*se* :	**os** escondéis	= You hide [yourselves].
acostar*se* :	**se** acuestan	= They, you (pol.) go to bed.

Note 1: Infinitive use: the reflexive pronoun corresponds to the subject:
(**Vosotros**) vais a vestir**OS** = You are going to get dressed.

Note 2: Verbs from the above list used non-reflexively:
Levanto *el brazo* = I raise my arm.
Acuesta *al niño* = He puts the child to bed.

2. Reciprocal meaning of the reflexive

Se envían cartas = They send letters *to each other*.
Se culpan (el uno al otro/mutuamente) = They blame *each other*.
(*But*: Se culpan a sí mismos = They blame themselves.)

3. Reflexive form in Spanish — but *not* in English

(a) Some verbs governing infinitives (§40) and objects (§51)
acordarse (de) : Me acordé de abrirlo = I remembered to open it.
olvidarse (de) : Se olvidó de los hechos = He forgot the facts.

(b) Changed meaning when reflexive, e.g.:

comer	=	to eat	comerse	=	to eat up
dormir	=	to sleep	dormirse	=	to go to sleep
hacer	=	to do/make	hacerse	=	to become
ir	=	to go	irse	=	to go away
poner	=	to put	{ ponerse	=	to put on (clothes); to become
			{ ponerse a	=	to begin to
volver	=	to return	volverse	=	to turn round

4. Position of reflexive pronouns:
See *Object Pronouns* (§12); *Imperative* (§38)

5. Special uses of the Reflexive:
To avoid the *Passive* (§46); with *parts of the body* (§25)

§57 SER AND ESTAR

SER: PERMANENT *basic features; unchangeable characteristics*	ESTAR: TEMPORARY *changeable states and conditions*
SER + adjective	*ESTAR + adjective*
El baúl **ES** rojo/grande/fuerte. = The trunk is red/big/strong.	El baúl **ESTÁ** vacío/lleno/cerrado. = The trunk is empty/full/shut.
La leche **ES** blanca. = Milk is white.	Esta leche **ESTÁ** agria. = This milk is sour.
ES malo = He is bad (= evil). Ella **ES** hermosa. (*an essential feature*) = She is beautiful.	**ESTÁ** malo = He is ill. ¿Cómo **ESTÁS** hoy? (*a variable* = *How are you today?* *condition*)
SER + noun or pronoun *Identity/existence/status*	*ESTAR: location/presence* (a) *Physical* (temporary and permanent).
ES inglés/profesor. = He is an Englishman/a teacher.	Los ingleses **ESTÁN** en el bar = The Englishmen are in the bar.
SOMOS nosotros = It is us. Madrid **ES** la capital de España.	**ESTAMOS** aquí = We are here. Madrid **ESTÁ** en España.
Possession, substance **ES** el mío = It is mine. La silla **ES** de plástico. = The chair is plastic.	(b) *Figurative* **ESTAMOS** en verano. = It is summer.
Number/time/facts Tres por tres **SON** nueve. Three times three equals nine.	¿A qué fecha **ESTAMOS?** **ESTAMOS** a tres de abril. (*But:* you may also say:
SON las cuatro = It is 4 o'clock.	¿Qué fecha **ES** hoy? **ES** el tres de abril)
El proyecto **ES** correcto. = The project is correct.	**ESTOY** en medio del proyecto. = I am in the middle of the plan.
SER + Past Participle: *The PASSIVE EVENT.*	*ESTAR + Past Participle:* *A STATE after the EVENT.*
Ayer, la fábrica **FUE** devastada por una gran explosión. = Yesterday, the factory was devastated by a huge explosion.	La fábrica **ESTABA** devastada, así que nadie podía trabajar allí. = The factory was destroyed, so nobody could work there.
SER + Infinitive	*ESTAR + Present Participle*
Trabajar **ES** ganar. To work is to earn. **Es** decir = That is to say.	**ESTOY** leyéndolo. = I am reading it. (See §52, *Progressive tenses*)

§58 SI CLAUSES

1. Simple Conditions: *fulfilment likely* — same tense as English.

Si pierde, le consolaremos = If he loses, we will console him.
Si me levantaba temprano, tomaba una ducha.
= If I got up early I would (= used to) have a shower.
Note: The *Future* and *Conditional* may only be used when **si** = whether:
Me pregunto si ganarán   = I wonder **whether** they will win.
Me preguntaba si ganarían = I wondered **whether** they would win.

2. Hypothetical or unlikely conditions — Subjunctive used, (§62)

Si + Imperfect Subjunctive	Conditional
Si *tuviese* la paciencia, = If I had the patience,	le toleraría. I would tolerate him.
Si + Pluperfect Subjunctive	**Conditional Perfect** (*or* **-ra** form Pluperfect Subjunctive)
Si lo **hubiera** hecho, = If he had done it,	lo habría (hubiera) admitido. he would have admitted it.

§59 SITTING AND STANDING

1. To sit down . . . sitting

Action — sentarse	me siento★ se sentó	= I sit down = He sat down	**Present** **Preterite**
State — estar + sentado	estoy sentado estaban sentados	= I am sitting = They were sitting	**Present** **Imperfect**

2. To stand up . . . standing

Action — levantarse	me levanto se levantó	= I stand up = He stood up	**Present** **Preterite**
State — estar de pie	estoy de pie estabais de pie	= I am standing = You were standing	**Present** **Imperfect**

★Do not confuse with sent**IR**, to be sorry; sent**IR(se)**, to feel:
  Lo siento = I am sorry. Me siento mal = I feel ill.

§60 SPELLING CHANGING VERBS: A SUMMARY

-AR VERBS	-CAR c → QU	-GAR g → GU	-ZAR z → C	-GUAR gu → GÜ
Preterite, *YO form only*	busQUé	lleGUé	reCé	averiGÜé
Pres. Subjunc. *throughout*	busQUe	lleGUe	reCe	averiGÜe

-ER & -IR VERBS	*consonant +* -CER, -CIR: c → Z	*vowel +* -CER, -CIR c → Zc	-GER, -GIR g → J	-GUIR gu → G	-QUIR qu → C
Pres, indic., *YO form only*	venZo, esparZo	conoZco, conduZco	coJo, diriJo	distinGo	delinCo
Pres. Subjunc. *throughout*	venZa, esparZa	conoZca, conduZca	coJa, diriJa	distinGa	delinCa

i and Y CHANGES	**Preterite,** *3rd persons*	**Imperf. Subjunc.** *throughout*	**Present Participle**
i → Y *-aer, -eer, -oer, -oír, -uir* e.g.: caer, leer, oír, huir	caYó caYeron	caYera caYese	caYendo
i removed: *-ñir, -llir, -eír* e.g.: gruñir, bullir, reír	gruñ __ ó gruñ __ eron	gruñ __ era gruñ __ ese	gruñ __ endo
y added to ⎰ Pres. Indic: *-UIR* verbs ⎱ Pres. Subj:	huYo, huYes, huYe, huimos, huís, huYen. huYa, huYas, huYa, huYamos, huYáis, huYan.		

Accent added to certain *-iar* and *-uar* verbs, and to *reunir* (§1.3)

---

§61 SUBJECT ↔ VERB AGREEMENT

1. Double subjects.

Ella y yo (= *we*) sal**imos** juntos = She and I leave together.

Tú y Juan (= *you* fam. plur.) salís juntos.
= You and John leave together.

2. Collective nouns

La gente quiere más = The people want more.
Todo el mundo busca la felicidad = Everybody looks for happiness.

La mayor parte del **ejercicio**   ES difícil.   (singular)

La mayoría de los **trenes**   VAN a Madrid.   (plural)

3. We English, you Spanish

Nosotros los ingleses **tenemos** un clima variable.
Vosotros los españoles **tenéis** un clima agradable.

§62 SUBJUNCTIVE MOOD

A. FORMATION OF THE SUBJUNCTIVE

1. Present Subjunctive

STEM + ENDINGS

-AR:	-e, -es, -e, -emos, -éis, -en
-ER	
-IR	-a, -as, -a, -amos, -áis, -an

(a) Regular: remove **-ar, -er** or **-ir** to form the stem
HABL -e, es, e, etc.   VEND -a, as, a, etc.   VIV -a, as, a, etc.

(b) Radical changing verbs

(i)   -AR and -ER types:
Same stem changes as the Present Indicative (§1)

pensar:	pIEnse, es, e	pensemos,	penséis	pIEnsen
perder:	pIErda, as, a	perdamos,	perdáis	pIErdan
contar:	cUEnte, es, e	contemos,	contéis	cUEnten
volver:	vUElva, as, a	volvamos,	volváis	vUElvan

(ii)   -IR type: note *nosotros* and *vosotros* forms:

sentir:	sIEnta, as, a	SINTamos,	SINTáis	SIEntan
dormir:	dUErma, as, a	DURMamos,	DURMáis	dUErman
pedir:	PIDa, as, a	PIDamos,	PIDáis	PIDan

(iii) jugar: juegue, es, a | juguemos,   juguéis | jueguen

(c) Spelling changing verbs

(i) -ar type

busCAR: c → qu busque, -es, -e, etc.	lleGAR: g → gu llegue, -es, -e, etc.	reZAR: z → c rece, -es, -e, etc.	averiGUAR: gu → gü averigüe, -es, -e, etc.

(ii) -er and -ir: stem provided by the **yo** form of the Present Indicative

coger	coJ	seguir★	SIG	conducir	conduZC
dirigir	diriJ	delinquir	delinC	conocer	conoZC
corregir★	CORRIJ	vencer	venZ	huir	huY
distinguir	distinG	esparcir	esparZ	argüir	arguY

e.g. coja, cojas, coja, cojamos, cojáis, cojan

★Note: *corregir* and *seguir* also have a radical change **e → i**

(iii) -iar/uar verbs; *reunir*: accent adopted as in Present Indicative

(d) Irregular verbs:
(i) Stem provided by **yo** form of the Present Indicative (§1.4)

caber	:	**quepa**	poder	:	**pueda**	traer :	**traiga**
caer	:	**caiga**	poner	:	**ponga**	valer :	**valga**
decir	:	**diga**	querer	:	**quiera**	venir :	**venga**
hacer	:	**haga**	salir	:	**salga**	ver :	**vea**
oír	:	**oiga**	tener	:	**tenga**		

(ii) Irregular stems   **(iii) Note the accents:**

haber	ir	saber	ser
HAYa	VAYa	SEPa	sea
HAYas	VAYas	SEPas	seas
HAYa	VAYa	SEPa	sea
HAYamos	VAYamos	SEPamos	seamos
HAYáis	VAYáis	SEPáis	seáis
HAYan	VAYan	SEPan	sean

dar	estar
dé	esté
des	estés
dé	esté
demos	estemos
deis	estéis
den	estén

2. Imperfect Subjunctive
Derived from the 3rd person plural of the Preterite (§5)

Remove **-RON** and add: $\begin{cases} \text{-ra, -ras, -ra, -ramos, -rais, -ran} \\ or, \text{ -se, -ses, -se, -semos, -seis, -sen} \end{cases}$

Examples

habla/**ron**	:	hablara or hablase
vendie/**ron**	:	vendiera or vendiese
vivie/**ron**	:	viviera or viviese

estuvie/**ron**	:	estuviera or estuviese
fue/**ron**	:	fuera or fuese
hubie/**ron**	:	hubiera or hubiese

3. Perfect Subjunctive

present subjunctive of haber: haya, -as, -a, -amos, -áis, -an	**+ past participle**

4. Pluperfect Subjunctive

imperfect subjunctive of haber:	
hubiera, -ras, -ra, -ramos, -rais, -ran★	+ **past participle**
or hubiese, -ses, -se, -semos, -seis, -sen	

★**Note 1:** The **-ra** forms of the Imperfect and Pluperfect Subjunctive may replace the Conditional and Conditional Perfect Tenses — see §10, §32, and §58

Note 2: The Imperfect Subjunctive forms **debiera** (§32) and **quisiera** (§49) are more polite than the conditional tense forms. Similarly with **poder**:

¿Puede	Podría	Pudiera usted	verme a las seis?
Can you	Could you	Could you possibly	see me at 6 o'clock?

B. EXAMPLES OF USAGE

1. After many expressions which *produce an effect on others*, but only where there is *a change of subject*, e.g.:

wishing	:	querer, desear	causing	:	hacer
asking	:	pedir, rogar	insisting	:	insistir en
telling to	:	decir	persuading	:	persuadir a
ordering	:	mandar, ordenar	advising	:	aconsejar
forbidding	:	prohibir, impedir	approving	:	aprobar, recomendar
allowing	:	permitir, dejar	preferring	:	preferir

Quiero que lo **olvides**	=	*I* want *you* to forget it.
Les dije que lo **terminara**	=	*I* told *them* to finish it.
Le pedí que lo **abriera**	=	*I* asked *him* to open it.
Impidieron que **se escapase**	=	*They* prevented *him* from escaping.

Note 1: *No change of subject?* — Use a simple infinive (see 10 below)

Note 2: *Decir* + indicative for facts:
Les dije que estaba terminado = I told them that it was finished.

Note 3: *To ask:* **preguntar** asks a question...
¿Quién viene? pregunté. Preguntó si yo tenía frío.
pedir: asks [to] somebody FOR something, see §51.

2. After expressions of emotion, e.g.:

sentir = to be sorry   alegrarse de que = to be glad
temer = to fear   estar contento de que = to be pleased.
Siento que usted haya perdido = I am sorry (that) you have lost.

3. After expressions of uncertainty

(a) Doubt, denial
Dudo que tenga veinte años = I doubt that he is twenty.
Negaron que estuviera roto = They denied that it was broken.
No es cierto que vengan = It is not certain that they are coming.

(b) Saying/believing in the negative
No creen que yo **tenga** éxito = They don't think I will succeed.
But indicative when affirmative: Creen que tendré éxito.

(c) Perhaps: *quizá(s)*, *acaso*, *tal vez*: Subjunctive if doubtful.
Quizás los **haya** traído = Perhaps he *may have* brought them.
But: Quizás los ha traído = Perhaps he has brought them (likely)

(d) Aunque: even if (*uncertain* ∴ *Subjunctive*); although (*certain* ∴
Indicative).
Aunque pierd**a** (uncertain) sonríe = Even if he loses, he smiles.
But: Aunque siempre pierd**e** (certain) sigue sonriendo.

4. After all impersonal expressions
(except *certainty*, e.g. es cierto que + indicative)

Es preciso que lo **traiga** = It is necessary that he brings it.
Es una lástima que **haya** fracasado = It is a pity he has failed.
Puede que **apruebe** = It is possible that he will (= He may) pass.

5. After these conjunctions:

para que   ⎫   sin que = without
a fin de que   ⎬ = in order that   con tal que = provided that
                ⎭   antes (de) que = before

a menos que   ⎫
a no ser que   ⎬ = unless
                ⎭
a condición de que = on condition that

Lo repararé antes (de) que **salgas** = I'll repair it before you go out.
Vendré con tal que todo **esté** preparado = I'll come provided that
everything is ready.

6. After these conjunctions *when referring to future time*:
cuando   = when   después (de) que = after
hasta que   = until*   en cuanto (que)   = as soon as
mientras   = while
Te telefonearé cuando/en cuanto (que) **sepa** las noticias.
I'll telephone you when/as soon as I know the news.

But: indicative for past or present time:
Te telefoneé cuando/en cuanto (que) supe las noticias.

*esperar a que + subjunctive = to wait until
Note also:
esperar que + subjunctive = to expect
esperar que + subjunctive = to hope
Espero que **estés** bien = I hope (that) you are well.
Esperas que **pague** yo? = You expect me to pay?

7. After negative and non-specific antecedents

No hallé **nada** que le **interesara** = I found nothing that interested him.
Busco __ una secretaria que **sea** bilingüe (no personal a: §48).
But: Indicative if the person is specific or known:
Empleé **a** una secretaria que **es** bilingüe.

Quienquiera que **sea, cualquier** (§22) **método** que adopte, y **por mucho** que **persista**, tengo miedo de que fracase.
= Who*ever* he is, what*ever* method he adopts and how*ever* much he persists, I fear that he will fail.

8. Imperatives and exhortations, §38.

Note also: ¡Ojalá! = If only...!
¡Ojalá pudiera entenderlo! = If only I could understand it!

9. Si Clauses, §58

10. Infinitive construction to avoid the subjunctive

(a) Clauses sharing the same subject Quiero **olvidarlo.** Lo reparé antes de **salir.**	**Compare:** *B.1 & 5 above*
(b) After: mandar, dejar, permitir, impedir, prohibir, aconsejar, ordenar, hacer e.g. Le impidieron **escaparse** = They prevented him from escaping.	*B.1 above*
(c) After impersonal expressions with no specific subject: Es preciso **traer**lo = It is necessary to bring it.	*B.4 above*

11. Sequence of Tenses

Main Clause	Subordinate Clause
Present, Perfect, Future, Imperative e.g. Le he pedido ...	Present or Perfect Subjunctive que lo termine.
Imperfect, Pluperfect, Preterite, Conditional. e.g. Le había pedido ...	Imperfect or Pluperfect Subjunctive. que lo terminara.

§63 TENER EXPRESSIONS

tener calor	= to be warm/hot	tener suerte	= to be lucky
tener frío	= to be cold	tener ____ años	= to be ____ years old
tener hambre	= to be hungry	tener éxito	= to be successful
tener sed	= to be thirsty	tener cuidado	= to be careful
tener miedo	= to be afraid	tener vergüenza	= to be ashamed
tener prisa	= to be in a hurry	tener que★	= to have to (See §32)
tener razón	= to be right	tener ganas de★	= to feel like
tener sueño	= to be sleepy	(★ + infinitive)	

Examples
Tengo dieciséis años = I am sixteen years old.
Tienen mucha hambre (f.) = They are very hungry.
Tenemos mucho calor (m.) = We are very hot.
¿Tienes ganas de probarlo? = Do you feel like trying it?

Note on temperature
Persons: *Tener + noun:* Tengo (mucho) frío = I am (very) cold.

Weather: *Hacer + noun:* Hace (mucho) calor = It is (very) hot. (§65)

Objects: *Estar + adjective*...a changed state (§57) —
          Mi comida está (muy) fría = My meal is (very) cold.
          Ser + adjective...inherent feature; "by definition" (§57) —
          El sol es (muy) caliente = The sun is (very) hot.

§64 TIME

1. El tiempo = time in a general sense (Also, *weather*, §65)

Pasé largo tiempo allí = I spent a long time there.
Llegamos a tiempo = We arrived on time.

2. La hora

    (a) = hour: He trabajado durante dos horas ... for two hours.

    (b) = appointed time:
La hora de levantarse = the time to get up.
Horas extraordinarias = overtime.
(c) Time of day: ¿Qué hora es? = What time is it?

ES la una*	= It is 1 o'clock
ES mediodía/medianoche	= It is 12 noon/midnight
Son las dos	= It is 2 o'clock
Son las tres y cuarto	= It is 3.15
Son las cinco y media*	= It is 5.30
Son las siete menos cuarto	= It is 6.45
Son las diez y veinte	= It is 10.20
Son las dos menos diez	= It is 1.50

Hora is feminine

It was	:	Era la una; eran las cinco.
Nearly	:	Son casi las dos.
About	:	A eso de las cinco *or* alrededor de las cinco.
Exactly	:	A las tres en punto.
To strike	:	Da la una. Daban las once.
		= It is striking one. = It was striking eleven.

a.m.	:	de la mañana; de la madrugada (early hours)
p.m.	:	de la tarde (until dark); de la noche (after dark)
un cuarto de hora	=	a quarter of an hour
tres cuartos de hora	=	three quarters of an hour
media hora más tarde	=	half an hour later

3. La vez = time (occasion)

una vez = once   dos veces = twice   muchas veces = often.
la próxima (última) vez = the first (last) time.

4. Expressions of time

today   = hoy
in the morning   = por la mañana
tomorrow (morning)   = mañana (por la mañana)
the day after tomorrow   = pasado mañana

yesterday (evening)   = ayer (por la tarde)
the day before yesterday   = anteayer
the day before   = el día anterior

last night   = anoche
the night before last   = la noche anterior/anteanoche

on Monday = el lunes   on Mondays = los lunes
every Monday = todos los lunes/cada lunes

next Sunday (year)   = el domingo (el año) que viene
last Sunday (year)   = el domingo (el año) pasado

Note these greetings:
Buenos días   (morning)
Buenas tardes   (after lunch/p.m.)
Buenas noches   (after dark/evening)
and ¡Hola!   (at all times)

§65 WEATHER

1. Hace: *It is* ... (Hacía = It was ...   Hará = It will be ...)

¿Qué tiempo hace?   Hace $\left\{ \begin{array}{l} \text{mal} \\ \text{buen tiempo.} \end{array} \right.$ Hace $\left\{ \begin{array}{l} \text{malo} \\ \text{bueno} \end{array} \right.$ (without tiempo)
= *What's the weather like?*   It is fine/bad.

Hace frío = It is cold   Hace viento = It is windy
Hace calor = It is warm   Hace fresco = It is cool
Hace sol   = It is sunny *But:* Está oscuro = It is dark
                             Está nublado = It is cloudy
(**Note: Hace** also means *ago* — see §37)

2. Hay = *It is*... (Había = It was ...   Habrá = It will be. §36)

Hay niebla = It is foggy   Hay sol = The sun is shining
Hay neblina = It is misty   Hay luna = The moon is shining.

3. Llover (*to rain*) **nevar** (*to snow*) **tronar** (*to thunder*) **helar** (*to freeze*)

Llueve todos los días = It rains every day   Present Tense
Está lloviendo ahora = It is raining now
Nevaba/Estaba nevando ayer = It was snowing yesterday (Imperfect)

§66 WORD ORDER

1. The order of subject and verb

(a) A matter of personal choice:

Mi hermano **llegó** ⎫
Llegó mi hermano ⎰ cuando me duchaba.

= My brother arrived while I was having a shower.

(b) Verb-subject order after direct speech:

-¡Le vi!- **exclamó** Juan.

(c) Interrogative form — the subject may be the last word:

¿Trabaja allí tu hermano? = Does your brother work there?
Or, tone of voice may indicate the interrogative:
¿Tu hermano trabaja allí?

Note: In Compound Tenses the subject follows both elements:
¿**Ha encontrado** usted las llaves? = *Have* you *found* the keys?

2. The object may precede the verb: it is then "*summed up*" in object pronoun form. (See §12.6)

3. See also: *Adverbs*, §23; *Imperatives*, §38; *Negatives*, §42.

INDEX

The references are to page numbers